PONS

Sprachlern-Comic Englisch

The Best of Both Worlds

von

Christianna Stavroudis und Alexander Schuch

PONS GmbH

Stuttgart

PONS

Sprachlern-Comic Englisch
The Best of Both Worlds
Comic-Sprachkurs zum Englischlernen

von
Christianna Stavroudis und Alexander Schuch

1. Auflage 2018

www.pons.de
E-Mail: info@pons.de

Projektmanagement: Angela de Riese
Logoentwurf: Erwin Poell, Heidelberg
Logoüberarbeitung: Sabine Redlin, Ludwigsburg
Einbandgestaltung: Anne Helbich
Comics und Illustrationen: Alexander Schuch
Satz: digraf.pl - dtp services
Druck und Bindung: Multiprint GmbH

ISBN: 978-3-12-562989-9

Willkommen!

Mit dem **Sprachlern-Comic Englisch** lernen Sie Englisch mit viel Spaß und Unterstützung durch eine Comic-Geschichte und zahlreiche Illustrationen.

So ist dieses Buch aufgebaut:

Jede Lektion beginnt mit einer **Auftaktseite**, auf der Sie erfahren, um welche Themen es in der Lektion geht.

Auf den nächsten Seiten lesen Sie dann im **Comic** die Geschichte von Nadeem und Sophie. In jedem Kapitel wird ihre Geschichte fortgesetzt.

Danach lernen Sie mit vielen Bildern den wichtigsten **Wortschatz** zum Thema der Lektion.

Im Abschnitt **Kommunikation** lernen Sie, was Sie in verschiedenen Situationen sagen können und wie Sie es sagen.

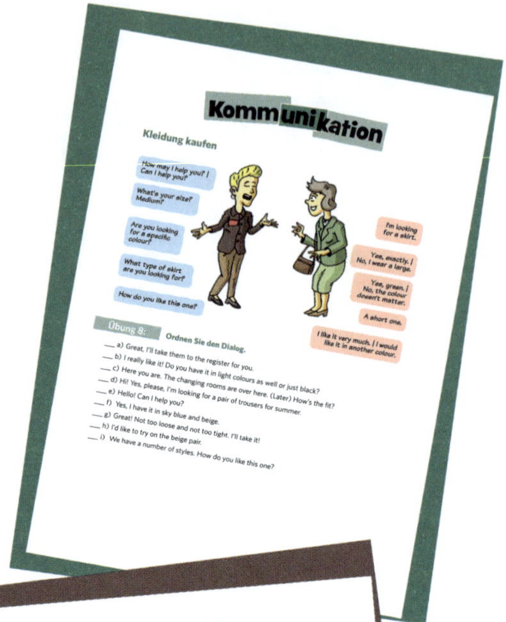

Danach geht es um die **Grammatik**, die Sie in diesem Teil lernen und üben.

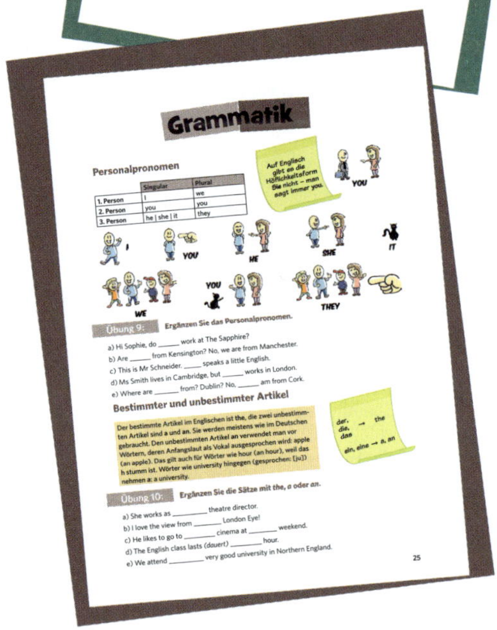

Im **Anhang** am Ende des Buches finden Sie die *Lösungen* aller Übungen. Außerdem gibt es hier eine *Wortliste* mit allen Wörtern aus dem Buch und eine *Liste der unregelmäßigen Verben*.

Viel Spaß und Erfolg beim Englischlernen!
Ihre PONS-Redaktion

Welcome

Anhang

I Welcome to London!

Wortschatz	Kommunikation	Grammatik
Länder und Sprachen Zahlen bis 100 Berufe	Persönliche Angaben Begrüßung und Abschied	Fragen Personalpronomen Präsens: Regelmäßige Verben und *to be* Satzstellung

HOTEL
Sapphire
Sapphire
TAXI
Good morning! Welcome to The Sapphire. How may I help you?
Hi, I have a reservation for Khan.
Ah yes, here it is. I need your personal information for validation, please.
Of course. My name is Nadeem Khan, my address is 7344 S Langley Avenue, Chicago, Illinois, USA...
Born on March 14th, 1981.
Thank you. That is all.
Name:
Nadeem Khan
Address:
7344 S Langley Avenue
Chicago, Illinois
USA
Date of birth:
14.03.1981
This is your keycard. Your room is 1505. It's on the 15th floor.
Great, thank you!

Could you show me the way to the elevator, please?
Certainly! The lift is right this way.
Here we are.
E
Oh, hello.
I hope you enjoy your stay, Mr. Khan.
It's off to a great start!

Hi, Dad! I made it to London. The weather's beautiful!
Yeah, Dad. Love you, too. Bye.
Uh... It's my first time in London, so I... uh...
Well, do you need any tips for the city?
I... As a matter of fact, I do.

We have plenty of sights.
For example, the London Eye...
Buckingham Palace...
Westminster Abbey...
And the Tower of London...
London is lovely!

The United Kingdom of Great Britain and Northern Ireland and the Republic of Ireland

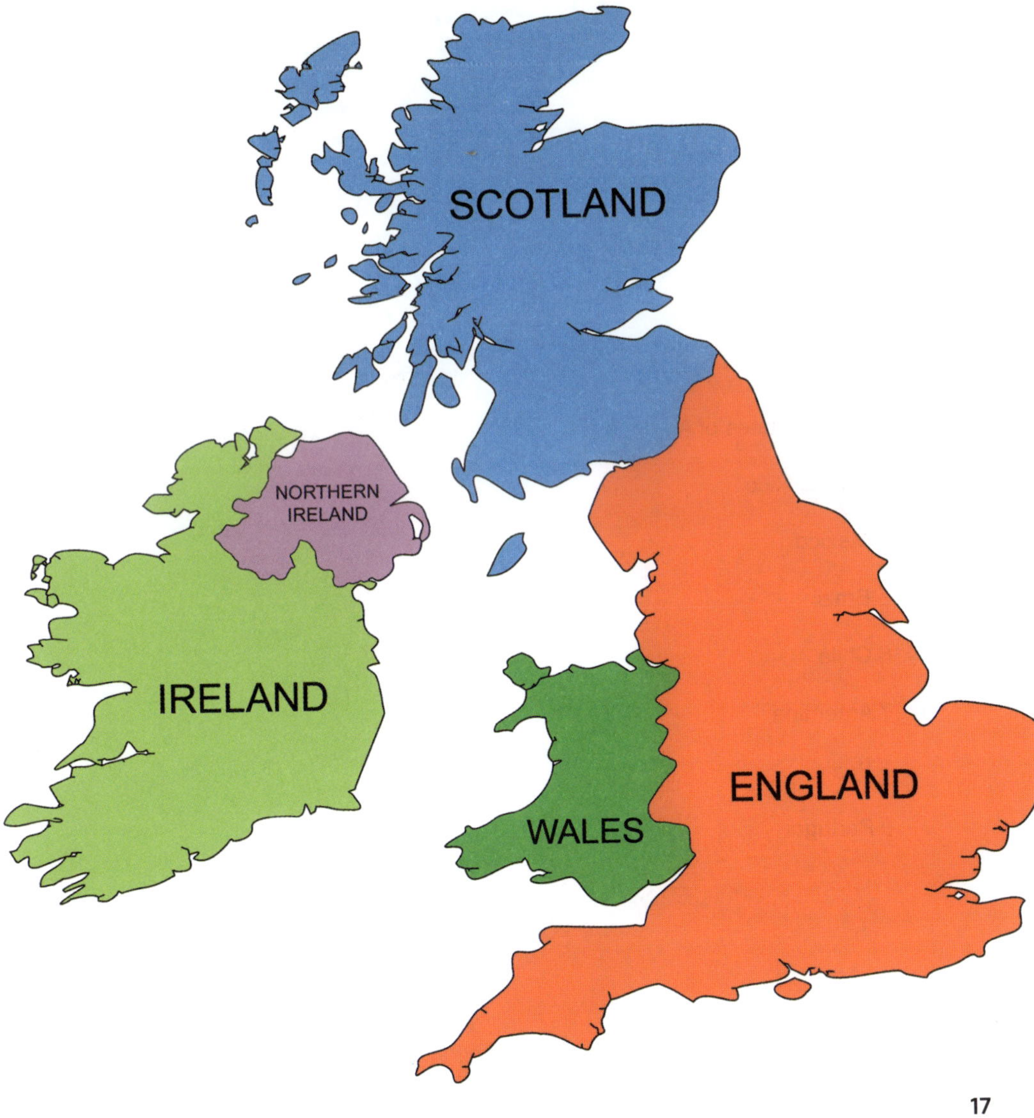

The world

1
2
3
4
5
6
7
9
1 Canada
2 United States of America
3 Puerto Rico
4 Mexico
5 Brazil
6 Chile
7 Argentina
8 Spain
9 Portugal

In den so markierten Ländern ist Englisch eine der offiziellen Amts- oder Landessprachen

Wortschatz

Länder und Sprachen

Im Englischen werden Nationalitäten meistens mit den Endungen **-n**, **-ian**, **-ish**, **-i** und **-ese** gebildet. Es gibt einige Ausnahmen.

-n: American (United States), German (Germany), Russian (Russia)
-ian: Canadian (Canada), Iranian (Iran), Norwegian (Norway)
-ish: British (Great Britain), English (England), Irish (Ireland), Spanish (Spain), Turkish (Turkey)
-i: Iraqi (Iraq), Pakistani (Pakistan)
-ese: Chinese (China), Japanese (Japan), Taiwanese (Taiwan)
Ausnahmen:
Czech (Czech Republic), Dutch (The Netherlands), French (France), Swiss (Switzerland)
Meistens stimmt die Nationalität mit dem Namen der Landessprache überein. Beispiele: Antonio is from Spain and speaks Spanish. Yi is from China and speaks Chinese. Fatima is from Pakistan and speaks Urdu and English.

Übung 1: **Woher kommen diese Menschen und welche Sprachen sprechen sie? Ergänzen Sie.**

a) Tomasz is from ________________. He speaks Polish.
b) Ove and Astrid speak ________________. They are from Norway.
c) Olga comes from Russia. She speaks ________________.
d) Dierk, Heidi and Johann speak German. They live in ________________, in ________________ and in ________________.
e) Zeynep and Mesut are from Turkey. They speak ________________.
f) Claire is from France. She speaks ________________.
g) Ai is from ________________. She speaks Japanese.
h) Enrique is from Mexico. He speaks ________________.

Zahlen bis 100

0 zero			
1 one	11 eleven	21 twenty-one	31 thirty-one
2 two	12 twelve	22 twenty-two	32 thirty-two
3 three	13 thirteen	23 twenty-three	…
4 four	14 fourteen	24 twenty-four	40 forty
5 five	15 fifteen	25 twenty-five	50 fifty
6 six	16 sixteen	26 twenty-six	60 sixty
7 seven	17 seventeen	27 twenty-seven	70 seventy
8 eight	18 eighteen	28 twenty-eight	80 eighty
9 nine	19 nineteen	29 twenty-nine	90 ninety
10 ten	20 twenty	30 thirty	100 one hundred

Übung 2: Suchen und markieren Sie die folgenden Zahlen.

1 - 4 - 11 - 12 - 15 - 16 - 20 - 55 - 61 - 72 - 80

A	F	O	U	R	N	A	E	U	W	G	O	P	X	S
U	D	N	O	F	I	F	T	E	E	N	I	H	P	E
B	F	E	F	N	I	O	W	K	S	A	V	J	R	V
S	C	W	B	I	Y	S	E	V	T	W	E	L	V	E
I	D	F	G	U	Q	I	N	O	Q	H	J	F	K	N
X	T	Z	A	D	V	X	T	L	S	A	D	E	L	T
T	R	N	F	I	F	T	Y	-	F	I	V	E	L	Y
Y	U	X	C	G	B	E	A	C	V	H	U	I	K	-
-	E	J	K	F	H	E	W	T	U	R	C	G	L	T
O	A	H	K	L	L	N	E	Z	I	O	G	H	K	W
N	V	C	E	U	M	C	G	D	G	H	N	T	E	O
E	D	F	J	K	I	E	L	E	V	E	N	Y	A	B

Übung 3: Lösen Sie folgende Matheaufgaben auf Englisch:

1. Twelve + fifteen = ______________
2. Thirty + ten = ______________
3. Eleven + seven = ______________
4. Eighty - twenty-three = ______________
5. One hundred - sixty-seven = ______________
6. Thirty - thirteen = ______________

Berufe

a painter

a greengrocer

a student

a policeman

a pensioner

a taxi driver, a cab driver

Kommunikation

Begrüßung und Verabschiedung

Saying hello:
Hello! My name is ... | My name is Sophie Robinson. (formell)
Hello! I'm Sophie. (informell)
Hi! How are you?

It is a pleasure to meet you! My name is Nadeem Khan. (formell)
Nice to meet you! I'm Nadeem. (informell)

Saying goodbye:
Goodbye! (formell)
Bye! (informell)
See you later! (informell)

Übung 4: Ordnen Sie den Dialog. Nummerieren Sie die Sätze von 1 bis 5.

___ a) No, I'm from Manchester, but I work in London.
___ b) Hello! I'm Thomas. What's your name?
___ c) I'm from London. And you? Are you also from London?
___ d) Nice to meet you. I'm Hannah.
___ e) Where are you from, Hannah?

Übung 5: Ergänzen Sie: pleasure | is | director | works | it's | happy

Fragen mit Fragewörtern: Who | What | When | Where | How

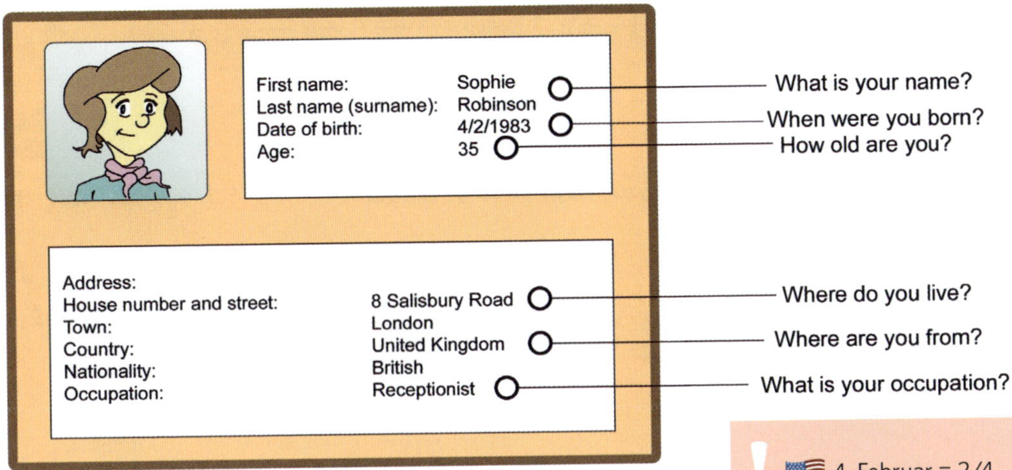

> ! 4. Februar = 2/4

Fragen mit Fragewörtern und *to be*

Fragen mit Fragewörtern und dem Verb **to be** (*sein*) werden ähnlich wie auf Deutsch gebildet:

Fragewort	Verb	Subjekt
Who (Wer)	**is** (ist)	**she?** (sie?)
What (Was)	**is** (ist)	**that?** (das?)

Yes-/No-Fragen

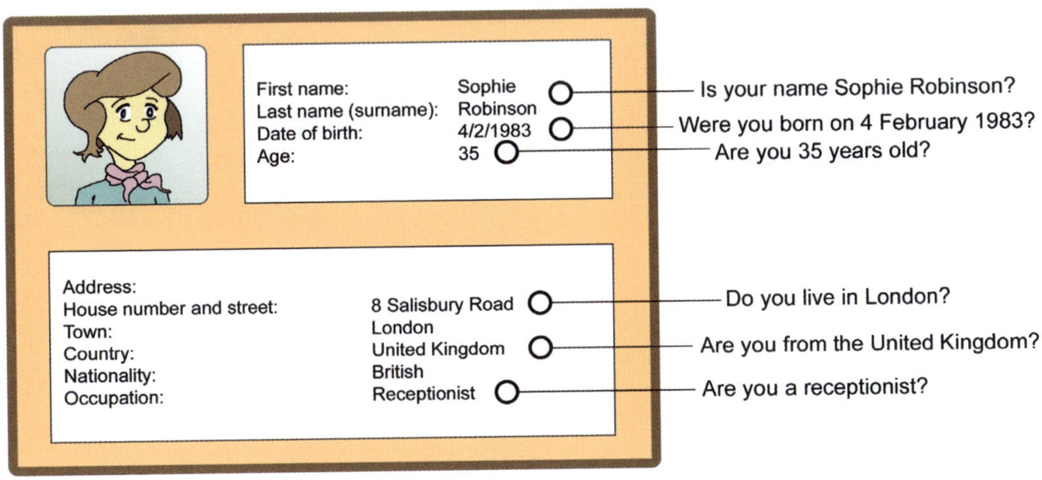

Übung 6: Bringen Sie die Sätze in die richtige Reihenfolge.

1. are | you | who | ? ____________________
2. it | what | is | ? ____________________
3. they | are | where | ? ____________________
4. you | how | are | ? ____________________

Übung 7: Ordnen Sie die richtige Antwort zu.

1. How old are you?
2. Where are you from?
3. Where were you born?
4. What are your names?
5. What is your native language?
6. Where do you live?
7. Who are you?
8. What is your address?

___ A I am from Slovakia.
___ B Our address is 8 Main Street.
___ C I live in Washington.
___ D I am 32 years old.
___ E I am Lucy.
___ F Our names are Anna and James.
___ G We were born in Hungary.
___ H My native language is German.

Übung 8: Füllen Sie das Bewerbungsformular mit Ihren eigenen Angaben aus.

First name:	
Last name (surname):	
Date of birth:	
Age:	
Address:	
House number and street:	
Town:	
Country:	
Nationality:	
Occupation:	

Grammatik

Personalpronomen

	Singular	Plural
1. Person	I	we
2. Person	you	you
3. Person	he | she | it	they

> Auf Englisch gibt es die Höflichkeitsform Sie nicht – man sagt immer you.

Übung 9: **Ergänzen Sie das Personalpronomen.**

a) Hi Sophie, do ______ work at The Sapphire?

b) Are ______ from Kensington? No, we are from Manchester.

c) This is Mr Schneider. _____ speaks a little English.

d) Ms Smith lives in Cambridge, but ______ works in London.

e) Where are _______ from? Dublin? No, ______ am from Cork.

Bestimmter und unbestimmter Artikel

Der bestimmte Artikel im Englischen ist **the**, die zwei unbestimmten Artikel sind **a** und **an**. Sie werden meistens wie im Deutschen gebraucht. Den unbestimmten Artikel **an** verwendet man vor Wörtern, deren Anfangslaut als Vokal ausgesprochen wird: apple (an apple). Das gilt auch für Wörter wie hour (an hour), weil das h stumm ist. Wörter wie university hingegen (gesprochen: [ju]) nehmen **a**: a university.

> der, die, das → the
>
> ein, eine → a, an

Übung 10: **Ergänzen Sie die Sätze mit *the*, *a* oder *an*.**

a) She works as __________ theatre director.

b) I love the view from ________ London Eye!

c) He likes to go to _________ cinema at ________ weekend.

d) The English class lasts *(dauert)* _________ hour.

e) We attend __________ very good university in Northern England.

Präsens: Regelmäßige Verben und *to be*

Die einfache Form der Gegenwart im Englischen nennt man **simple present**. Sie ist wirklich sehr einfach, denn im Gegensatz zum Deutschen wird im Englischen nur die 3. Person Singular (he/she/it) konjugiert, alle anderen Formen bleiben wie im Infinitiv. Für die Form in der dritten Person Singular wird an das Verb die Endung **-s** angehängt.

to come: he, she, it comes

auch: to ask, to like, to work, to eat

Bei wenigen Verben wird statt **-s** die Endung **-es** angehängt:

to do: he, she, it does

auch: to go (goes), to teach (teaches)

Achtung, beim Verb **do** ändert sich in der 3. Person Singular die Aussprache:
I do [du]
he does [daz]

Das Verb **be** (*sein*) ist unregelmäßig:

I am (I'm)	we are (we're)
you are (you're)	you are (you're)
he, she, it is (he's, she's, it's)	they are (they're)

Bei den Formen in Klammern handelt es sich um Kurzformen, die in der gesprochenen Sprache sehr häufig verwendet werden.

Übung 11: Ergänzen Sie das Verb in der richtigen Form.

a) I __________ from Hungary. (*to come*)
b) __________ you French? (*to be*)
c) Amal __________ Arabic. (*to teach*)
d) Peter __________ English, German and a little Spanish. (*to speak*)
e) We __________ in Ireland. (*to live*)
f) They __________ from Spain. (*to be*)
g) Janice __________ to the café. (*to go*)

Übung 12: Ergänzen Sie:

to be | to speak | to work | to live in | to come from

a) Robert is 39 years old.
b) He __________________ Manchester.
c) He __________________ England.
d) His last name __________________ Cooper.
e) He __________________ as a language teacher.
f) He __________________ English, Spanish and a little French.

Übung 13: Schreiben Sie einen Text wie im Beispiel.

Name and age: Ewa Nowak, 27
Country of birth: Poland
Town of residence: Aberdeen
Occupation: fashion designer
Languages: Polish, English, German

*My name is Ewa Nowak. I am 27 years old and come from Poland.
I live in Aberdeen and work as a fashion designer.
I speak English, Polish and German.*

And you?

Name: ______________________
Country: ______________________
Town/place of residence: ______________________
Occupation: ______________________
Languages: ______________________

My name is ______________________
____
____
____

Wortstellung: Aussage- und Fragesätze

Aussage	Sophie lives in London.
Frage mit Fragewörtern	Where does Sophie live?
Ja-/Nein-Frage	Does Sophie live in London?
Ja-/Nein-Frage mit **to be**	Is Sophie a secretary?

Übung 14: Schreiben Sie die Sätze in der richtigen Reihenfolge.

a) from | you | come | Italy | do | ? *Do you come from Italy?*
b) native language | what | your | is | ? ______________________
c) surname | my | is | Williamson | . ______________________
d) speak | German | does | she | ? ______________________
e) Glasgow | in | do | live | you | ? ______________________
f) English | I | speak | a little | . ______________________

2 Nadeem and his family

Wortschatz	Kommunikation	Grammatik
Familie und Verwandtschaft Farben In der Natur In der Stadt	Über die Familie sprechen Hobbys	Plural der Nomen Present progressive Possessivartikel

Nadeem's story begins in 1980 in Pakistan.
Ghazala, we're moving to the United States!
GREENCARD
CHICAGO
KARACHI
They quickly move from Karachi to Chicago to start a new life.
It's a boy!
And shortly after their arrival, little Nadeem arrives, too.
Khan's
Grand opening!
In the spring of 1981, they open up their own grocery store.

Isn't she beautiful?
Two years later, Nadeem's sister Nadia is born.

In 1984, Ghazala gets a job as a saleswoman in a boutique.

In 1986 little Nadeem starts school.

He's a very good student, and always pays attention.
Boing

After school, he plays basketball or helps out his father at work.
Wack

Nadeem, could you help me out over here?
Nom
Nom

And sometimes the Khans visit their grandmother in Karachi during the summer.
Hi, mother! Good to see you again.

After high school, Nadeem leaves for college and studies marketing and sales.

Great Lakes
Mike, we have a meeting with a client this afternoon...
After graduation, he gets a position at Great Lakes Industries. Now he's the director of sales!

Nadia decided to study veterinary medicine to help sick and injured animals.
Meow.

Wortschatz

Wasim and Gazala are married: they are **husband** and **wife**. They are **father** and **mother** to two **children**, one **son** and one **daughter**: Nadeem and Nadia. Nadeem's **sister** Nadia is married to Farid and they have two children as well: Nadeem's **nephew** Karim and his **niece** Sarah. Nadeem and Nadia's **grandmother** lives in Pakistan.

Farben

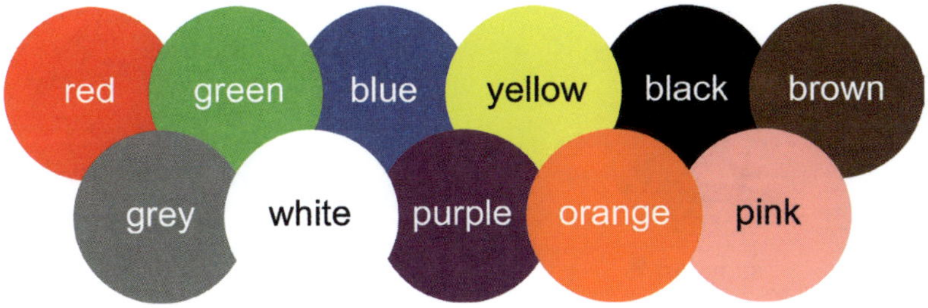

In der Natur

In der Stadt

Übung 1: Welches Wort passt?

grass | yellow | blue | sun | sky | trees | white

a) The ______________ is blue. A bird is flying. It is also ______________.

b) The clouds are ______________, and the ______________ is yellow.

c) The meadow and the ______________ are green. The ______________ are also green.

d) There is a flower in the meadow. It is white and ______________.

Übung 2: Nennen Sie die Farben der Flaggen des jeweiligen Landes.

a) United Kingdom ______________________________

b) Ireland ______________________________

c) Scotland ______________________________

d) Wales ______________________________

e) Germany ______________________________

Die vier Jahreszeiten

spring

summer

autumn

winter

! Summer is my favorite time of the year.
ABER: I like to travel in **the** summer.

! autumn = fall

Übung 3: Ergänzen Sie mit spring, summer, autumn/fall, winter

a) What is ____________ like? – It's not very warm.
The leaves are changing colour and falling.

b) When do the first flowers start to appear?
In ________________.

c) What is ____________ like? – Much is covered in white.
It's cold.

d) ___________ in London is often hotter than people think.
The sun is shining.

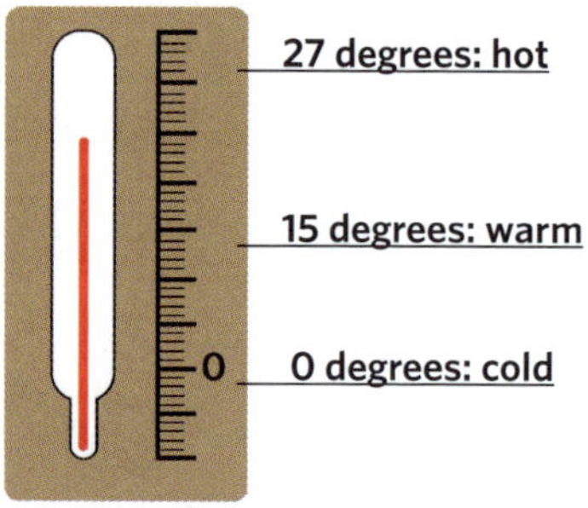

! In den USA wird die Fahrenheit-Temperaturskala verwendet.
0 °C = 32 °F, 10 °C = 50 °F, 20 °C = 68 °F, 30 °C = 86 °F, 40 °C = 104 °F

Kommunikation

Über Familie sprechen

Übung 4: Ordnen Sie die passenden Antworten zu.

1. Do you have brothers and sisters?
2. Are you married?
3. Do you have a large family?
4. How often do you see your nephew?
5. Do you have children?

a) No, I'm single.
b) No, I have a small family.
c) Yes, I have a daughter. She's one year old.
d) Not often. He lives is Scotland.
e) Yes, one brother and one sister.

Marital status:

single

married

divorced

Übung 5: Beantworten Sie die Fragen.

1. Do you have any children? If so, how many and what are their names?
2. Where do your parents live?
3. What are your mother's hobbies?
4. What is your father's favorite colour?
5. Do you have any brothers or sisters or are you an only child?

Hobbys

Do you have a hobby?
What do you like to do?
What do you do in your free time?

Yes, I play the guitar.
I like to learn languages.
I like riding my bike in my free time.

like + -ing-Form: Jemand tut etwas tatsächlich und genießt es.

like + to + Infinitiv: bezieht sich auf eine Option, die nicht unbedingt auch ausgeführt wird.

to go cycling

to dance

to play football

to play the guitar

to read

to paint

Übung 6: Ordnen Sie den Dialog.

___ a) You're an artist? And what do you paint? Flowers?
___ b) Yes, I like to dance in my free time. Do you?
___ c) Do you do any sports?
___ d) Sorry, but I hate football. I prefer listening to music. And I paint.
___ e) No, houses and streets. Do you like to dance?
___ f) No, I can't move well to music, but I like to listen it.
___ g) Yes, I play football. And you? Do you play football in your free time?

Übung 7: Und was machen Sie in Ihrer Freizeit? Schreiben Sie ein paar Sätze dazu.

In my free time I ____.

Grammatik

Plural der Nomen

Regel	Pluralendung	Beispiele
Um den Plural, also die Mehrzahl eines Substantivs zu bilden, hängt man in den meisten Fällen ein **-s** ans Ende.	-s	cloud → clouds tree → trees flower → flowers
Wenn das Substantiv auf *s*, *x*, *z*, *ch* oder *sh* endet, hängt man **-es** an, um die Pluralform zu bilden.	**bei s, x, z, ch:** -es	bus → buses box → boxes church → churches dish → dishes
Wenn das Substantiv auf *y* endet, wird das *y* mit der Pluralendung zu *i*, die Endung lautet also **-ies**.	**bei y:** -ies	sky → skies pony → ponies baby → babies
Und natürlich gibt es auch einige Ausnahmen.	unregelmäßig	woman → **women** man → **men** child → **children** foot → **feet** person → **people** leaf → leaves mouse → **mice** life → lives potato → potatoes diagnosis → diagnoses

one **person** → many **people**

Übung 8: Bilden Sie die Pluralform.

a) city - ____________
b) star - ____________
c) bird - ____________
d) wish - ____________
e) sandwich - ____________
f) life - ____________
g) gas - ____________
h) tax - ____________

Present Progressive

Es gibt zwei Formen der Gegenwart im Englischen: das **Present Progressive** (auch Present Continuous genannt) und das **Simple Present**. Das Simple Present haben Sie bereits in Kapitel 1 kennengelernt. Das Present Progressive ist die Verlaufsform. Man benutzt sie, um unvollendete Abläufe zu beschreiben, die jetzt im Moment passieren und auch, wenn man über feste Pläne oder Vereinbarungen spricht. Z. B.: **Manuel Neuer plays for Germany but he is not playing football right now.**

Present Progressive kann auch als informelle Futurform verwendet werden: **Are you doing anything fun this weekend? - Yes, we're going to an amusement park with the kids.**

Das Present Progressive wird aus der Präsensform von **be** und der -ing-Form des Verbs gebildet:

She	**is**	**reading.**
Subjekt	to be	Infinitiv + -ing

Bei der **Verneinung** wird **be** verneint:

She	**isn't**	**reading.**
Subjekt	to be + not	Infinitiv + -ing

Bei Fragen wird die Form von **be** nach vorne gestellt, danach folgt das Subjekt und dann die -ing-Form.

Is	**she**	**reading?**
to be	Subjekt	Infinitiv + -ing

Übung 9: Bilden Sie Sätze im Present Progressive.

a) When ______________________ *(you, go)* to Dublin this summer?
b) What ______________________ *(Sophie, do)* later?
c) She ______________________ *(go out)* with friends.
d) What ______________________ *(film, play)* at the cinema this weekend?
e) I ______________________ *(not, read)* many books right now.

Übung 10: Simple Present oder Present Progressive?

a) I ________________ to read novels *(to like)*.
b) Right now, I ________________ a really good thriller *(to read)*.
c) Nadeem ________________ no children *(to have)*.
d) How are you enjoying the party? I ________________ a great time! *(to have)*

Übung 11: Beantworten Sie die Fragen.

1. What are you currently reading?
2. We're going to a music festival.
3. Are you learning any other (andere) languages right now?
4. Jane Eyre by Jane Austen.

a) No, only English.
b) Where are you going this weekend?
c) Yes, I'm seeing my friends at a class reunion soon.
d) Are you meeting with friends soon?

Possessivartikel

Possessivartikel kommen vor dem Substantiv und drücken Zugehörigkeit aus (mein, dein, sein etc.).

I → my you → your he → his she → her it → its	we → our you → your they → their

Achtung!
it's = it is
its = Possessivartikel von it

Übung 12: Ergänzen Sie:

your | her | my | his | our | their

a) We live at Oxford Street 8. ________ house is yellow.
b) My father has a new hobby. ________ hobby is football.
c) Hello, Mr Robinson! Is that ________ dog? No, it's not ______ dog.
d) Is that Sophie's mum? No, that's ________ aunt.
e) Sophie and Nadeem live in the city. ________ apartments are small.

3

Asking Sophie out

Wortschatz	Kommunikation	Grammatik
Wochentage Zahlen ab 100 Jahreszahlen Monatsnamen Ordnungszahlen Datum	Aktivitäten in der Stadt Pläne machen Die Uhrzeit	Will future Objektpronomen Temporale Präpositionen Modalverben Negation would like/want

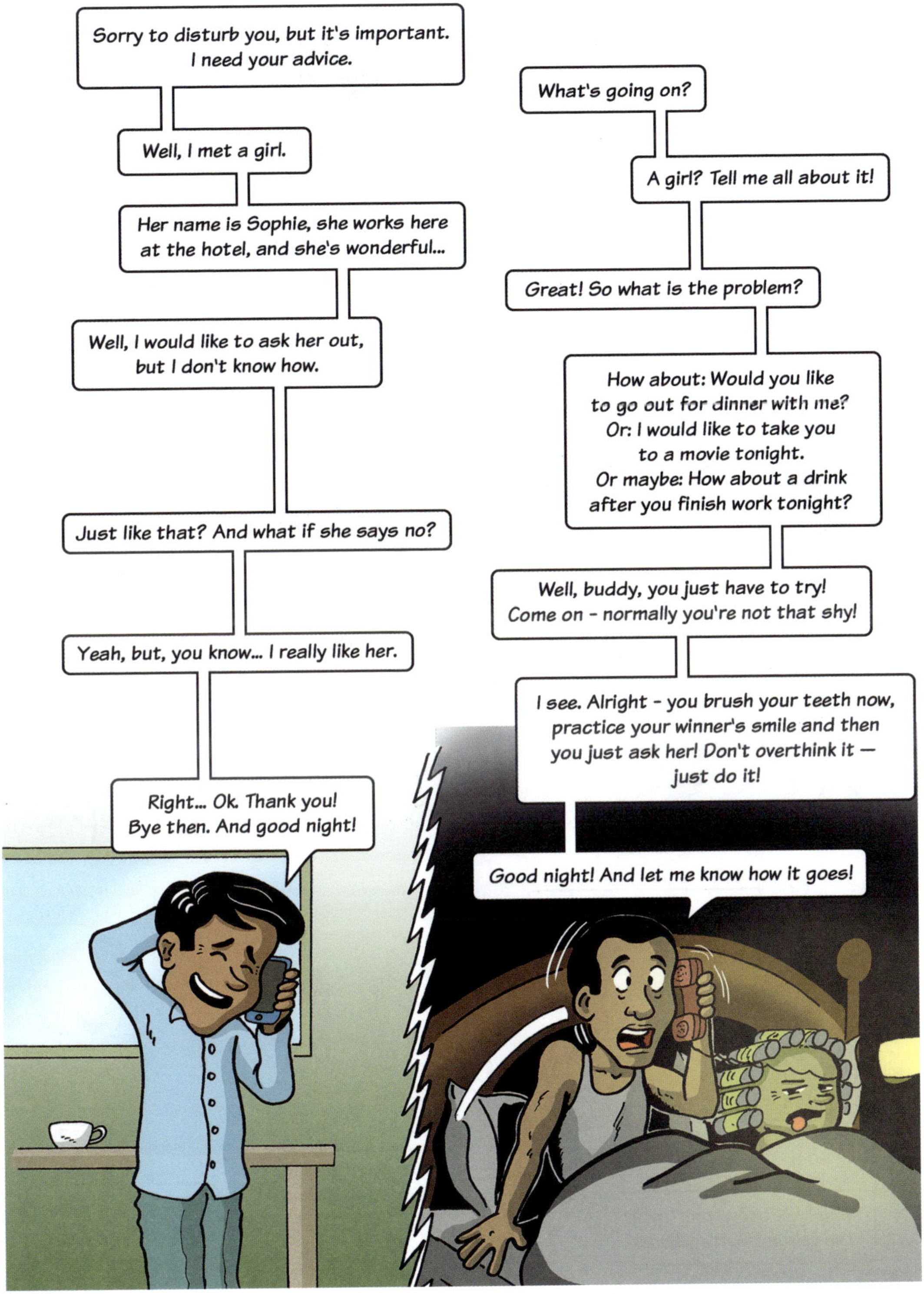
Sorry to disturb you, but it's important. I need your advice.
What's going on?
Well, I met a girl.
A girl? Tell me all about it!
Her name is Sophie, she works here at the hotel, and she's wonderful...
Great! So what is the problem?
Well, I would like to ask her out, but I don't know how.
How about: Would you like to go out for dinner with me? Or: I would like to take you to a movie tonight. Or maybe: How about a drink after you finish work tonight?
Just like that? And what if she says no?
Well, buddy, you just have to try! Come on – normally you're not that shy!
Yeah, but, you know... I really like her.
I see. Alright – you brush your teeth now, practice your winner's smile and then you just ask her! Don't overthink it – just do it!
Right... Ok. Thank you! Bye then. And good night!
Good night! And let me know how it goes!

The Sapphire, hello. How may I help you? Yes, we have a room available. When are you checking in?
Hi, um... I was wondering which Tube, um, I can use to get to the exhibition?
Oh, that's easy, take the Piccadilly. It takes you all the way to the exhibition and back!
Oh, great!.. Good to know... Say, um... Could I perhaps... um... take you out some time?
I'd love to!
Really? That's great! How about tonight?
No, I have to work late.
How about tomorrow?
Tomorrow I have to stay at the fair until after dinner.
Do you have time Thursday afternoon?
Thursday is good, I'm off at 3pm.

Fantastic! Would you like to go to the movies? Or have dinner? Maybe go for a walk?
Wait, how about the London Eye?
To be honest, I'm a little afraid of heights, but...
Me too, but the view is unbeatable!
Let's meet at the café next to Morton's Tower at 4 pm. We can have a cup of coffee there and it's only a short walk to the London Eye.
Sounds like a plan.
I'm looking forward to it. See you on Thursday!
Bye!
Yes!
Joe:
Hey, how did it go?
Me:
Great!!! Thanks for the advice! Date on Thursday at 4 pm. Wish me luck!

Wortschatz

Wochentage

the weekend

the week
Monday, Tuesday, Wednesday, Thursday, Friday, Saturday, Sunday

When?
(an dem kommenden oder vergangenen Tag oder Wochenende) **On** Monday | **During** the week | **At** the weekend
(wenn es sich um jede Woche handelt) **On** Mondays | **On** weekdays. / **During** the week. | **At** weekends. / **At** the weekend.

the day
Today is Sunday.
Yesterday was Saturday.
The day before yesterday was Friday.
Tomorrow is Monday.
The day after tomorrow is Tuesday.

Übung 1: **Ergänzen Sie die Wochentage.**

a) Sophie works five days a week, from ______________ to ______________. She's free at the weekend.

b) Today is Friday. Tomorrow is ______________ and I can sleep in. The day after tomorrow is ______________ and my parents are coming over for brunch.

Zahlen ab 100

100	a hundred/one hundred
200	two hundred
300	three hundred
713	seven hundred and thirteen
1,000	one thousand
2,000	two thousand
1,000,000	one million
1,000,000,000	one billion
1,000,000,000,000	one trillion

Jahreszahlen

Jahreszahlen:

142 = one hundred and forty-two
500 = five hundred
1100 = eleven hundred
1200 = twelve hundred
1800 = eighteen hundred
aber
1000 = one thousand
2000 = two thousand

Für die ersten neun Jahreszahlen jedes Jahrhunderts außer beim jetzigen Jahrhundert wird eine Null wie der Buchstabe „o" ausgesprochen. Bei den zweiten bis elften Jahrhunderten ist das „o" optional.

801 = eight "o" one - oder - eight hundred and one
1006 = ten "o" six - oder - a thousand and six
1208 = twelve "o" eight
1903 = nineteen "o" three
aber
2007 = two thousand and seven

Für die anderen Jahreszahlen jedes Jahrhunderts:

1228 = twelve twenty-eight
1973 = nineteen seventy-three
2017 = twenty seventeen
Bei den zweiten bis elften Jahrhunderten ist das optional:
710 = seven ten - oder - seven hundred and ten
245 = two forty-five - oder - two hundred and forty-five

Übung 2: **Schreiben Sie die (Jahres-)Zahlen aus.**

a) 780 ____________________
b) 1,056 ____________________
c) 1700 (year) ____________________
d) 1808 (year) ____________________
e) 1837 (year) ____________________
f) 2011 (year) ____________________

Monatsnamen

1986

January	February	March
April	May	June
July	August	September
October	November	December

the year
When? In 1986.
the month
When? In July

Ordnungszahlen

Die Ordnungszahlen im Englischen, also 4., 5., 6. usw., werden normalerweise gebildet, indem man -th an das Zahlwort anhängt, z.B. four → four**th**. Einige Zahlen weichen dabei in der Schreibung etwas ab, wie Sie in der Liste unten sehen.
Die ersten drei Zahlen haben ganz eigene Formen:

one → first (1st),
two → second (2nd),
three → third (3rd)

Das gilt auch für alle zusammengesetzten Zahlen mit 1, 2, 3, also für 21-23, 31-33 usw.

fourth	seventh	tenth
fifth	eighth	eleventh
sixth	ninth	twelfth
		thirteenth

Datum

Today is the first of May.

Today is May first.

Übung 3: Schreiben Sie das Datum wie im Beispiel.

Bitte entscheiden Sie sich für die britische oder amerikanische Variante und kreuzen Sie an:
☐ britisch ☐ amerikanisch

What is today's date?

a) (01/12) Today is the first of December. Today is December first.
b) (05/04) ______.
c) (11/11) ______.

When are you leaving for Dublin?

d) (27/02) I am leaving for Dublin on the twenty-seventh of February. I am leaving for Dublin on February twenty-seventh.
e) (02/07) ______.
f) (18/06) ______.

When were you born?

g) (08/03/1952) I was born on the eighth of March nineteen fifty-two. I was born on March eighth nineteen fifty-two.
h) (31/01/1996) ______.
i) (03/10/2002) ______.

Kommunikation

Aktivitäten in der Stadt

1. to go to a restaurant | to eat out
2. to go to a café
3. to go to the cinema | to go to the movies
4. to go to a concert
5. to go to the gym
6. to go to the pub | to go for a drink

Übung 4: **Zu welcher Aktivität passt das? Schreiben Sie die Nummer.**

___ a) to do sport

___ b) to watch a film/movie

___ c) to go for a beer/pint

___ d) to listen to live music

___ e) to have a coffee, to have a piece of cake

Pläne machen

Shall we go to the cinema tomorrow?
Would you like to go to the cinema tomorrow?

Yes, great idea! Yes, I would love to!
No, I'm sorry. I don't have time.
Sorry, I can't. I have to work.

When shall we meet? At 6 o'clock?
How's 6 o'clock? Is 6 OK?

Yes, that's great | perfect!
No, that's too late.
Could we meet earlier? | at five o'clock?
How about five o'clock?
No, that's too early.
Could we meet later ?| at seven o'clock?
How about seven o'clock?

Übung 5: **Ordnen Sie den Dialog von 1 bis 6.**

___ a) See you tomorrow!

___ b) Sorry, that's too early. How about 7 o'clock?

___ c) Yes, that's perfect! See you tomorrow, then!

___ d) Sure. When does the concert start?

___ e) Hi, Silvia! There's a concert tomorrow evening at the park. Would you like to go with me?

___ f) At 8 o'clock. Shall we meet at Café Royal at 6 o'clock?

Die Uhrzeit

Zeit	USA	GB
10:15	quarter after 10	quarter past 10
9:45	quarter of 10	quarter to 10
10:30	ten-thirty	half-ten/half past ten

Excuse me, what time is it? | Do you have the time?

It's three o'clock | three thirty/half past three | three forty-five/a quarter to four.

At what time | When shall we meet up?

At three o'clock (sharp) | three thirty/half past three | three forty-five/a quarter to four

Im Englischen wird die 24-Stunden-Zählung nur in offiziellen Kontexten (z.B. Ansagen am Flughafen oder Bahnhof) gebraucht. Im täglichen Leben sowie bei der Arbeit werden alle Uhrzeiten zwischen Mitternacht und 11:59 am Vormittag mit den Zahlen von eins bis zwölf und dem Zusatz **a.m.** angegeben, alle Uhrzeiten von zwölf Uhr mittags bis 23.59 Uhr mit den Zahlen von eins bis zwölf und dem Zusatz **p.m.**

a.m. = (früher) Morgen
p.m. = Nachmittag, Abend, Nacht

! 12:00 a.m. = midnight (0:00)
12:00 p.m. = noon (12:00)

formell: three o'clock
informell: three o'clock sharp | on the dot

3 "o" five (siehe Notiz zu Jahreszahlen)
five past three

three ten
ten past three

three fifteen
(a) quarter past three

three twenty-five
twenty-five past three

three thirty
half past three

three thirty-five
twenty-five to four

three forty-five
(a) quarter to four

three fifty-five
five to four

Übung 6: Schreiben Sie die informelle Uhrzeit.

a) Shall we meet at the cinema at (5:50 p.m.) ________ this evening?
b) When does the concert start? At (8:15 p.m.) ________.
c) The bus departs at (10:40 p.m.) ________ in the (morning/evening) ____________.

Grammatik

Will future

Wie Sie im Gespräch im Comic zwischen Sophie und Nadeem gesehen haben, drückt Nadeem seine Absicht, Sophie um 16 Uhr abzuholen, mit **I'll pick you up** aus. **I'll** ist die Kurzform von **I will** und deutet auf Versprechungen für die Zukunft. Die Verneinung lautet entweder **will not** oder **won't** (beide Varianten haben dieselbe Bedeutung). Das Hilfsverb **will** und auch seine Verneinung haben für alle Personen dieselbe Form.

-Can you come to the concert Friday night?

-I'll be there and I won't be late!

-Are you two coming to Sarah's birthday party?

-Yes, we'll bring the champagne!

Übung 7: **Ergänzen Sie den Dialog.**

have | do | sounds | see | I'll | will | looking

Hey! ___________ you have time for a drink after work this Thursday?

Sorry, I ___________ to work late, but how about Friday night? There's a street food festival in the East End. Tim and Jonathan ___________ be there, too.

___________ great! ___________ pick you up at the office at 6.

Thanks! See you then. I'm ___________ forward to it ☺.

Objektpronomen

In folgender Tabelle sehen Sie die Personalpronomen im Nominativ (engl. „subjects"), die Sie schon aus dem ersten Kapitel kennen, und die entsprechenden Objektpronomen.

Subjekt (Nom.)	**I** (ich)	**you** (du)	**he** (er)	**she** (sie)	**it** (es)	**we** (wir)	**you** (Sie; Ihr)	**they** (sie)
Objekt (Akk.)	**me** (mich / mir)	**you** (dich / dir)	**him** (ihn / ihm)	**her** (sie / ihr)	**it** (es / ihm)	**us** (uns)	**you** (Sie / Ihnen; euch)	**them** (sie / ihnen)

Übung 8: Ordnen Sie die richtige Antwort zu.

a) Do you know this man?
b) Do you know Mr and Mrs Khan?
c) Do you know Café Royal?
d) Do you know Sophie Robinson?

___ A Yes, I know it well.
___ B No, we don't know him.
___ C Yes, I know them.
___ D Yes, of course we know her!

Übung 9: Ergänzen Sie.

us | me |them | her | it

1. When are you meeting up with your friend? I'm meeting up with ______ the day after tomorrow.
2. Do you have the tickets with you? Yes, I have ________.
3. Do you love ________? Yes, of course I love you!
4. There's a bird in that tree! Do you see ______?
5. Tom and Sally are taking ______ with them to the concert Friday night. We're so lucky!

Temporale Präpositionen: on, at, in, from...to...

When is the concert?	The concert is ... on Monday |on 12 May 2017. in May | in the summer | 2019. at half past seven.	 on + Wochentag | Datum in + Monat | Jahreszeit | Jahr at + Tageszeit
When is the ice cream parlor open?	The ice cream parlor is open ... from Monday to Saturday. from April to September. from 10 a.m. to 7 p.m.	from ... to ...

Übung 10: Schreiben Sie die richtige Präposition.

a) _____ August we are going to Italy on holiday.
b) The First World War ended _____ 11 November _____ 11 a.m.
c) I work ______ 8:30 a.m. _____ 4:30 p.m.
d) We love to go to the cinema ______ the winter.

Modalverben

can (können) | could (könnte) | must (müssen) | may (dürfen) | have to (müssen) | should (sollen)

Bei Modalverben im Englischen bleibt die Stammform für alle Subjektpronomen (auch die 3. Person Singular) gleich. Das heißt:

✓ he/she can, must, has to, could, may, might, should

✗ ~~he/she cans, musts, coulds, mays, shoulds~~

Negation (Verneinung) with *not*

- I am not/I'm not German. I'm Austrian. (mit dem Verb „to be")
- I am not/I'm not eating (mit present progressive)
- I cannot come tonight. (mit Modalverben: can, may, might must, have to, shall ...)
- I do not like television. (mit allen anderen Verben)

I	am	not	German.	
I	am	not	eating	
I	can/may	not	come	tonight.
I	do	not	like	television.

must/have to = müssen

You must / have to go to the Florida Keys! They're stunning!

must not / mustn't = nicht dürfen

You mustn't eat on the tube.

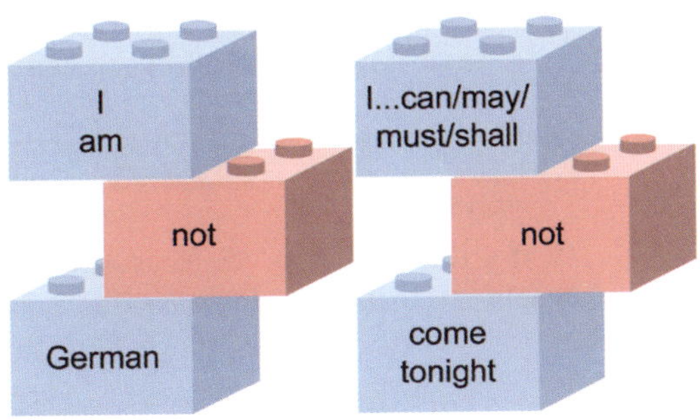

Übung 11: Beantworten Sie die Fragen in vollständigen Sätzen.

a) Do you have children? ______________________________.
b) Are you going to a concert on Sunday? ______________________________.
c) Do you have a cat? ______________________________.
d) Do you have to work today? ______________________________.
e) Are you eating out tonight? ______________________________.
f) Do you like coffee? ______________________________.
g) Do you work out every day? ______________________________.

Sentence order with modal verbs (Satzordnung) mit Modalverben:

	Modalverb	Infinitiv		
She	can	play	the violin	Aussage
She	can't	play	the violin	Aussage (negativ)

Modalverb		Infinitiv		
Can	she	play	the violin?	**Ja-/Nein-Fragen**

> **!** Bei negativen Aussagen mit Modalverben kommt don't/doesn't nie vor.
> ✗ She ~~doesn't can~~ play the violin.

	Modalverb		Infinitiv		
When	can	she	play	for us?	**W-Fragen**

		Modalverb		Infinitiv		
How	well	can	she	play	the violin?	**Fragen mit Fragewort „how"**

Übung 12: Übersetzen Sie die Aussagen bzw. Fragen ins Englische.

a) Er kann Gitarre spielen. ______________________________.
b) Wie viele Sprachen kann sie sprechen? ______________________________?
c) Wann sollten wir am Bahnhof sein? ______________________________?
d) Könntest du bitte das Fenster zumachen? ______________________________?
e) Mama, darf ich mit meinen Freunden spielen? ______________________________?

Übung 13: Welches Modalverb passt? Bitte ankreuzen.

a) I ☐ **can't** ☐ **may not** ☐ **must not** go to the gym this evening. I have to work late.
b) They really ☐ **may not** ☐ **should not** ☐ **could not** eat so many cookies if they want to lose weight.
c) ☐ **Must** ☐ **Could** ☐ **May** you please call me back?
d) ☐ **Should** ☐ **Must** ☐ **Could** we please pay the bill?

Would like (to) | want (to)

Wenn man um etwas bittet, benutzt man **would like**. Es ist unhöflich, **I want/we want** zu sagen. Wenn man einen Wunsch ausspricht, der keine Bitte ist, reicht **want**, aber auch **would like** ist richtig.
Michael would like/wants an ice cream.
Oder: Michael would like to have/wants to have an ice cream.

And what would you like to drink, young man?

I want lemonade!

Don't you mean "I would like lemonade?"

I want to live in a world where nobody goes to bed hungry.
I want you to be happy.

Übung 14: Ergänzen Sie die Formen.

a) **On the phone:** Good morning! I w______________ to speak to Mr Thompson.
b) **Two friends at the cinema:** Which film should we see? – I really w____________ to see a classic film.
c) **At the pub:** Good evening! What can I get you? – I w______________ a pint of bitter, please.
d) **A father and his two sons, Ben and Max:** Come on, boys. Time for bed. – But I w__________ to stay up and watch TV! And Max w_____________ to watch TV, too!

4 What's he like?

Wortschatz	Kommunikation	Grammatik
Aussehen und Charakter Kleidung	Kleidung kaufen Über Kleidung und Farben sprechen	Die Verben *like, love, hate, prefer* Verstärkende Adverbien

So, tell me more about this Nadeem guy. What is he like?
Cafe Flair
He's tall, has dark hair, brown eyes and comes from the States. He works for Great Lakes Industries.
Go on!
Well, he's actually very shy, polite, intelligent... and really handsome!
Sounds like a great catch!
Hello, ladies. What'll you have?
I'd like to have a coffee with milk and sugar, please.
And a cappuccino for me, please.
Lydia, I can't tell you how excited I am.
I'll bet he feels the same way, believe me.
Oh dear, but I don't think I have anything to wear.

We should go shopping then. Don't worry: I'm a fashion expert.
Here you are. One coffee and a cappucciono.
Thank you. We'd also like the bill, please.
Of course, that'll be 4.20 pounds.
Keep the change.
Thank you and have a nice day.
Do you think this will work? I want to look pretty.
Darling, we will make you irresistible.
Cheers to that!

MM
% SALE
This store's not bad. I usually find something in there.
Let's check it out.
50%
Look at all these great clothes! I think I'll try on a skirt. Or maybe a dress? Stripes or dots? Can you hold this for me, please?
Sophie, do you even know your size? Sophie? Are you listening to me?
I'm sorry, did you say something?
Do we have enough now? This stuff is getting heavy...
Oops...

Honey, I think the dots might not be the best choice...
You look stunning, but it's a little too much for a first date.
Fabulous piece, but I think fur is out of fashion...
Wait a minute, I didn't choose this. What's the big idea? I look like a farm boy!
Well... What do you think?
I think we found what we're looking for. Let's take it!

Wortschatz

Aussehen und Charakter

Der Körper:

Haare und Gesicht:

Charakter:

Übung 1: Der perfekte Mann. Ergänzen Sie.

He works out and takes care of his b________________.

He's t_________ and m____________.

He has s_________, b___________ hair and green e____________.

He likes to laugh and tells good jokes. He's f____________.

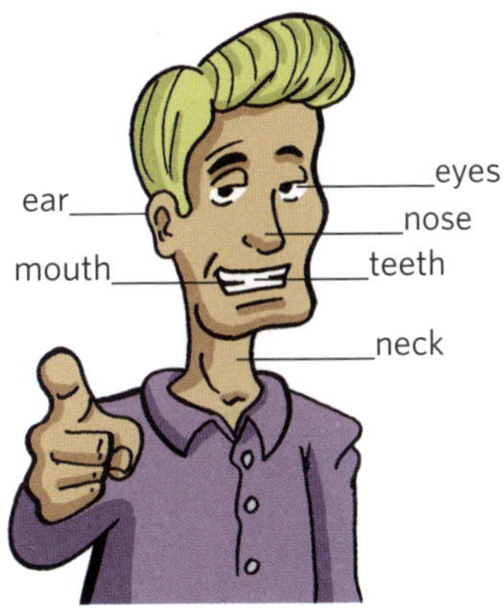

Übung 2: Wer bin ich?

1. I have brown hair, wear a beard, and often have a top hat on. I'm the sixteenth president of the United States. Who am I? ______________________________
2. I have blond hair and often wear red lipstick. I'm the star of famous movies like *The Seven Year Itch* and *How to Marry a Millionaire*. Who am I? ______________________
3. I'm bald and the star of the Die Hard films. Who am I? __________________________
4. My nickname is "Old Blue Eyes". My famous songs are "New York, New York" and "Fly Me to the Moon". Who am I? _____________________
5. I have grey hair and wear glasses. I often wear a black turtleneck, blue jeans, and white trainers. People know me for my invention, the iPhone. Who am I?

   ____

Übung 3: Beschreiben Sie eine Ihrer Lieblingspersönlichkeiten.

____

____

____

Übung 4: Ergänzen Sie:

dull | funny | long | muscular | serious | skinny | slim | tall | teeth

1. I need to go to the hairdresser *(Friseur)*. My hair has got too ______________.
2. David is so _________________! He goes to the gym every day.
3. You should laugh *(lachen)* more and not be so ___________________.
4. Anne is ___________ and _____________, but she was ______________ when she was a kid.
5. Jennifer has beautiful white _______________ and a great smile.
6. I didn't like the movie at all. It was really ______________. I prefer ______________ comedies.

Kleidung

jacket
t-shirt
jeans
cap
purse
blouse
skirt
blazer/jacket
shirt
tie
belt
suit
trousers
shoe
dress
hat
scarf
winter coat
mitten
boot
polo shirt
shorts
sock

Übung 5: Was trägt man ...? Schreiben Sie die Wörter.

At the weekend, in the summer:

a) I like to wear OHSRTS ____________ and a STRIT-H ____________.

In the winter:

b) We wear warm OTOSB ____________, a long ATCO ____________, TIMTNSE ____________, a HTA ____________, and a RACFS ____________.

Formal wear at the office:

c) Women often wear a LUEBSO ____________ and a RITKS ____________ or a pair of USORTRSE ____________.

d) Men often wear a dark UTIS ____________, a HRTIS ____________, and a ETI ____________.

Übung 6: Wie heißt das Gegenteil? Ergänzen Sie mit Adjektiven aus dem Kasten.

plain | ugly | short (x2) | cheap | old | dull | loose | skinny | dark | old-fashioned | uncomfortable

a) long ____________
b) tight ____________
c) light ____________
d) expensive ____________
e) new ____________
f) interesting ____________
g) tall ____________
h) colorful ____________
i) fat ____________
j) modern ____________
k) comfortable ____________
l) beautiful ____________

Übung 7: Was ist das Problem? Schreiben Sie das passende Adjektiv.

a) The jumper doesn't fit. It's too ____________.

b) The trousers are too ____________.

c) The bag is too ____________.

d) And the shoes are far too ____________!

Kommunikation

Kleidung kaufen

Übung 8: **Ordnen Sie den Dialog.**

___ a) Great, I'll take them to the register for you.

___ b) I really like it! Do you have it in light colours as well or just black?

___ c) Here you are. The changing rooms are over here. (Later) How's the fit?

___ d) Hi! Yes, please, I'm looking for a pair of trousers for summer.

___ e) Hello! Can I help you?

___ f) Yes, I have it in sky blue and beige.

___ g) Great! Not too loose and not too tight. I'll take it!

___ h) I'd like to try on the beige pair.

___ i) We have a number of styles. How do you like this one?

Über Kleidung und Farben sprechen

green
yellow
red

purple
multi-coloured
blue
light blue
dark blue

black
white
brown
beige

pink
orange

Do you like to wear
Do you like
How do you like

blouses
shirts
skirts
jeans
the colour red
colourful socks
?

Yes, very much.
No, I prefer t-shirts.
It's/they're bright | beautiful | ugly | comfortable | too uncomfortable.
I like it/them very much.
It's/they're alright. I don't like it/them very much.

Übung 9: **Und Sie? Was tragen Sie (nicht) gerne? Schreiben Sie Sätze.**

In the summer | In my free time | At the office I like to wear ...
I like | I don't like ...
What clothing is beautiful | elegant | boring | unfashionable?

Grammatik

Die Verben *like, love, hate,* und *prefer*

Um Vorlieben und Abneigungen auszudrücken, kann auf die englischen Verben **like** (mögen), **love** (lieben), **hate** (hassen) und **prefer** (bevorzugen) entweder der Infinitiv oder das Gerundium folgen. Das Gerundium wird mit der Endung **-ing** gebildet. In vielen Fällen gibt es keinen Bedeutungsunterschied zwischen dem Infinitiv und dem Gerundium:

I like to wear dresses. = I like wearing dresses.
Nadeem prefers to go to the movies. = Nadeem prefers going to the movies.

Bei **love** und **hate** kommt das Gerundium häufiger vor, da diese Verben starke Gefühle über Tätigkeiten im Allgemeinen ausdrücken:
We love shopping!
They hate doing homework!

Die Höflichkeitskonstruktion **would like** erfordert hingegen immer den Infinitiv und nie das Gerundium:
Would you like to go out at the weekend?
Nadeem would like to see Sophie again.

Übung 10: **Was mögen Sie? Was mögen Sie nicht? Schreiben Sie Sätze.**

I like to ______________________________.
I prefer to ______________________________.
I hate ______________________________.

Verstärkende Adverbien

Wörter wie **too** (zu), **very** (sehr), **really** (wirklich), **rather** (ziemlich) und **quite** (recht) kann man in Kombination mit Adjektiven benutzen, um diese zu verstärken.
He's very good at languages.
The red dress is really beautiful.

Manche Adjektive drücken schon eine Intensität aus, die keine weitere Verstärkung erlaubt.
He's excellent at languages.
The red dress is gorgeous.
You look stunning!

Übung 11: **Beantworten Sie die Fragen.**

1. Is the cake tasty? No, it's ____________________ *(zu süß)*.
2. Do the trousers fit well? No, they are ____________________ *(zu eng)*.
3. Do you like my friend? Yes, she's ____________________ *(sehr nett)*.
4. Do you like my haircut? It's ____________________ *(recht kurz)*.
5. Are you enjoying the music? - No, it's ____________________ *(ziemlich laut)*.

5 Working from 9 to 5

Wortschatz	Kommunikation	Grammatik
Tätigkeiten im Alltag Frühstück	Im Café Mit dem Auto oder zu Fuß?	Adjektive: Steigerung Vergleiche mit *as* und *than* Stellung der Häufigkeitsadverbien Das Verb *get* Phrasal verbs Verben *have, make, take, do*

Sophie's day begins at 8 a.m. Time to get up!
Nadeem has to get up even earlier at 6 a.m.
06:00
Sophie starts by eating breakfast and reading the newspaper.
Nadeem takes a shower, brushes his teeth and gets dressed for work. This takes about 20 minutes.
After breakfast, Sophie takes a shower, puts on her makeup, and gets dressed. That takes over 30 minutes.
Nadeem jumps into his car at 6:30 and heads off to work.

Then she usually cleans her flat, or walks into town to buy groceries.
Before reaching work, Nadeem stops at a fastfood restaurant to get a breakfast sandwich and a big cup of coffee...
Sophie's lunchtime is directly at noon.
...which he consumes on his way to work.
She takes a tube line at 12:30 to get to work.
Nadeem starts working at 7:30, checking his emails and going through his appointments.

Sophie starts work at 1 p.m. As a receptionist, she takes calls, plans bookings, and takes care of the guests' needs.
Nadeem has to attend many meetings during the week, discussing plans, pitching ideas and consulting the sales program.
Often Sophie has to juggle answering emails and phone calls at the same time.
At 1 p.m. Nadeem goes out with his colleagues for lunch.
If she has the time, Sophie likes to take a coffee break together with her colleagues.
Great Lakes
On a good day, Nadeem can leave work by 6 p.m.

Sophie leaves work at 9 p.m. Time to wrap it up and call it a day.
O-Mart
Before heading home, he often goes shopping at the supermaket.
Before she goes to bed, Sophie likes to read a few pages of her book...
In the evening, Nadeem often has a snack and watches sports on TV. Or he goes jogging with a friend.
But she usually falls asleep at 11 p.m.
At 10:30 p.m. Nadeem finally goes to sleep.
22:30

Wortschatz

Tätigkeiten im Alltag

Übung 1: **Was machen Sie zuerst? Und danach? Nummerieren Sie.**

___ a) eat lunch/take a lunch break ___ b) fall asleep

___ c) go to work ___ d) go home ___ e) shower and eat breakfast

___ f) wake up ___ g) go to bed ___ h) eat dinner

What's for breakfast?

Übung 2: **Schreiben Sie die Wörter zu den Bildern.**

1. ______________

2. ______________

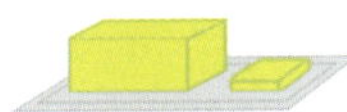
3. ______________

4. ______________

5. ______________

6. ______________

7. ______________

8. ______________

9. ______________

10. ______________

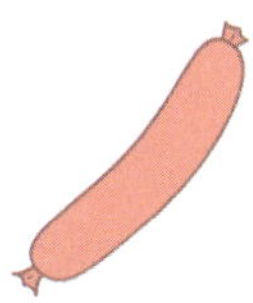
11. ______________

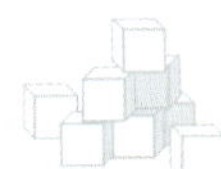

12. ______________

bread | butter | cheese | coffee | egg | honey | jam | milk | roll | tea | sausage | sugar

Gewohnheiten: how long? how often?

How long?

How long does that take? How long does it take you to ...?	It takes | I'll need ... It takes me (*Zeitangabe*) to ...
How long do you need?	just a minute| 5 minutes | half an hour (30 minutes) | two hours

How late?

How late do you work?	Until 5:00 p.m. |Until the late afternoon.

Übung 3: **Schreiben Sie die Antworten.**

a) How long do you need in the bathroom in the morning? – *I need* ________________.

b) How long does it take you to get to work? ________________.

c) How late do you work on Fridays? ________________.

d) How late do you sleep in at the weekend? ________________.

Übung 4: **Was machen Sie wie oft? Schreiben Sie.**

cook | eat breakfast | watch television | listen to the radio | read a book |
read the newspaper | go dancing | work out/exercise

I listen to music every day, but I rarely go dancing.

____

____

always

Mo	Tu	We	Th	Fr
X	X	X	X	X
X	X	X	X	X
X	X	X	X	X

regularly | every day |
every Wednesday

Mo	Tu	We	Th	Fr
		X		
		X		
		X		

often | frequently

Mo	Tu	We	Th	Fr
	X	X		
X			X	
				X

sometimes

Mo	Tu	We	Th	Fr
	X			
			X	

seldom | rarely

Mo	Tu	We	Th	Fr
			X	

never

Mo	Tu	We	Th	Fr

Kommunikation

Im Café

Im englischsprachigen Ausland wird nur selten getrennt bezahlt. Stattdessen regelt man die Rechnung unter sich und zahlt zusammen oder man lädt den anderen ein und wird das nächste Mal eingeladen.

! In den USA erwartet die Bedienung ein Trinkgeld in Höhe von 15% des Rechnungsbetrags. Bei sehr gutem Service ist ein Trinkgeld in Höhe von 20% üblich.

Café Flora

Breakfast menu (until 11:00 a.m.)

French breakfast
(croissant with jam or honey)

Full English breakfast (bacon, eggs, fried tomatoes, mushrooms, bread and sausage)

Coffee or tea

Lunch menu

Savoury sandwiches

Soup

Mineral water, cola, beer, wine

Übung 5: Wer sagt was? Die Bedienung oder der Gast? Kreuzen Sie an.

	waiter	guest
a) With cheese, please.	☐	☐
b) Would you like to pay with cash or card?	☐	☐
c) Shall I bring you the breakfast menu?	☐	☐
d) Would you like to have something to eat as well?	☐	☐
e) Hello! What would you like to drink?	☐	☐
f) I'm sorry, we don't serve breakfast after 11:00 a.m.	☐	☐
g) No, thank you. I would only like a coffee.	☐	☐
h) Do you accept credit cards?	☐	☐
i) With or without gas?	☐	☐
j) May I have the wine menu, please?	☐	☐
k) A coffee with milk and sugar, please.	☐	☐

Mit dem Auto oder zu Fuß?

How do you get to the train station? To work? Back home?

I go on foot.

I take the bus / go by bus.

I ride my bike.

bus

bicycle | bike

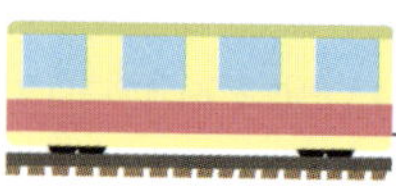
train

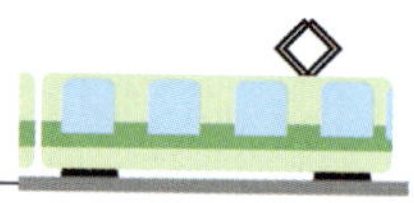
tram

underground

on foot

on foot | by train | by bike | by bus | by car (Auto fahren = drive)	go
the bus | my bike | the train | the tram | the underground	ride
the bus | the train | my bike | the tram the underground	take

Übung 6: Welche Antwort passt? Ordnen Sie zu.

a) Do you drive to work?
b) How do you usually travel to Norfolk?
c) Do you prefer taking the underground or riding your bike to university?
d) How long does it take you to get to work?
e) How do you get home in the winter?

___ A I drive to the train station and take the train at 3:54 p.m.
___ B Twenty minutes by bike and half an hour on foot.
___ C In the winter we take the bus or the tram.
___ D No, I go on foot. My office is very close by.
___ E I prefer riding my bike.

Übung 7: Und Sie? Schreiben Sie drei Sätze.

a) To get to work, I ____________________.

b) To get to the supermarket, I ____________________.

c) In the wintertime, I ____________________.

Übung 8: Ergänzen Sie die Sätze.

a) I wake up every __________ at seven __________.

b) I get up, __________ a shower and get dressed.

c) Then, I ______ __________. I drink a cup of coffee and read the __________.

d) I go to the bus stop and __________ the bus to work. It takes half an __________.

e) I arrive at the __________ at 8:30 a.m. and work until noon.

f) Then I have __________ with my colleagues.

g) In the __________ I work until 5:30 p.m.

h) After work, I usually go directly __________.

i) Sometimes, I buy __________ at the supermarket.

j) I'm then home at 7:00 p.m. I cook something and eat __________.

k) Then, I relax a bit and __________ telly.

l) At 10:00 p.m. I go to __________.

afternoon | bed | dinner | groceries | home | hour | lunch | make breakfast | morning | newspaper | o'clock | office | watch | take x 2

Übung 9: Interview zu Ihrem Tagesablauf. Schreiben Sie die Antworten.

a) When do you get up every morning?
b) When do you have breakfast?
c) What time do you get to work | to university | to school?
d) How late do you work every day?
e) How long is your lunch break?
f) When do you usually get home?
g) What do you make for dinner?

____

____

____

____

____

____

____

Grammatik

Adjektive: Steigerung

Doris is big and fat.

Bessie is bigger and fatter.

Ruby is the biggest and the fattest.

Regelmäßige Formen (bei einsilbigen Adjektiven):

Grundform	Komparativ	Superlativ
small big sad huge dry	smaller bigger sadder huger drier	smallest biggest saddest hugest driest

Bei einsilbigen Adjektiven mit kurzem Vokal wird der Konsonant verdoppelt: big → bigger

Endet das Adjektiv auf -e, wird nur -r und angehängt: rude → ruder, nice → nicer

Wenn das Adjektiv auf Konsonant plus -y endet, dann wird -y zu -ier (shy → shier). Dies gilt auch für zweisilbige Adjektive.

Regelmäßige Formen (bei zweisilbigen Adjektiven):

Die Steigerung für zweisilbige Adjektiven folgt entweder dem „-er, -est"-Muster oder dem „more, most"-Muster. Hier gibt es leider keine allgemeine Regel: Man sollte diese Informationen für jedes zweisilbige Adjektiv in einem Wörterbuch nachschlagen.

Grundform	Komparativ	Superlativ
happy healthy clever	happier healthier cleverer/more clever	happiest healthiest cleverest/most clever

Regelmäßige Formen (bei drei- oder mehrsilbigen Adjektiven):

Grundform	Komparativ	Superlativ
expensive beautiful	more expensive more beautiful	most expensive most beautiful

Unregelmäßige Formen:

Grundform	Komparativ	Superlativ
good bad much	better worse more	best worst most

Alle Adjektive, egal wie viele Silben, die auf -ful, -less, -ing, -ed, und -ous enden, bilden den Komparativ und Superlativ mit **more** und **most**.

Grundform	Komparativ	Superlativ
bored boring hopeful hopeless	more bored more boring more hopeful more hopeless	most bored most boring most hopeful most hopeless

Übung 10: **Ergänzen Sie:**

funniest | nicest | warmest | longer | better | more | faster | warmer

a) Everyone is funny in my family, but my father is the ____________________.

b) These shoes cost a lot, but these boots cost ________________.

c) It's warm in June, ______________ in July and _______________ in August.

d) Daniel is good at video games, but Claire is even ________________.

e) I'm fast on my bike, but I'm _______________ with my car.

f) It takes a long time to get home, but it takes _______________ with traffic.

g) Michael is simply the ________________ man I know!

Vergleiche mit *as* und *than*

Rose is *as* big *as* Doris.

Ruby is bigger *than* Rose and Doris.

Übung 11: **Ergänzen Sie mit *as* oder *than*.**

a) I like drinking tea as much _____ coffee.

b) I would rather have a roll ______ toast at breakfast.

c) Do you think long hair is as beautiful ____ short hair?

d) Danny speaks French better ______ his sister.

e) My husband sleeps in longer _______ I do at the weekend.

Stellung der Häufigkeitsadverbien

Im Gegensatz zu Adverbien der Zeit (z.B. yesterday, tomorrow) oder Adverbien des Ortes (z.B. here, over there) stehen Häufigkeitsadverbien direkt vor dem Vollverb.

I often play golf on Sunday.
We rarely go on picnics.
I'm always thinking of you.

Wenn das Vollverb das Verb *to be* ist, steht das Adverb nach dem Verb:

Janet is often in the countryside on the weekend.
You are always late!

Folgende Häufigkeitsadverbien können aber auch entweder am Anfang oder am Ende des Satzes stehen: frequently (häufig), normally (normalerweise), occasionally (gelegentlich), often (oft), sometimes (manchmal), und usually (meistens).

I go swimming frequently.
Sometimes I read the newspaper.
Usually I'm home by 8:00 p.m.

Übung 12: **Bilden Sie Sätze.**

1. meat | she | eats | never ______________________.
2. TV | he | watches | rarely ______________________.
3. on time | they | always | are ______________________.
4. rarely | dancing | go | I ______________________.
5. go | to the movies | he | frequently ______________________.
6. poetry | write | she | sometimes ______________________.

Das Verb *get*

Dieses Verb kommt in der informellen gesprochenen Sprache häufig vor und hat verschiedene Bedeutungen:

I can get you the skirt in another size. (get = holen)
Many children get pocket money from their parents. (get = bekommen)
She is getting angry now. (get = werden)
You're getting taller every year! (get = werden)
(present progressive wird hier benutzt, weil der Ablauf des Böse- bzw. Großwerdens betont wird.)
Children! It's time to get dressed! (get dressed = sich anziehen)
I should get new shoes. (get = kaufen)
How do you get home from work every day? (get = kommen, gelangen)

Übung 13: **Übersetzen Sie folgende Sätze mit get ins Englische.**

1. Jetzt werde ich richtig böse!

   ______________________!
2. Im Winter wird es dunkler und kälter.

   ______________________.
3. Ich muss Milch und Brot im Supermarkt holen.

   ______________________.
4. Mit jedem Jahr wird mein kleiner Bruder größer.

   ______________________.
5. Wie kommt man dahin?

   ______________________?

Phrasal verbs

Phrasal verbs kommen auch in der gesprochenen Sprache häufig vor und bestehen aus einem Verb und einem Partikel:
Every morning she gets up at 6:30 a.m.
At the weekend, I sleep in until 8:00 a.m.

Manche phrasal verbs mit Objekten können nach dem Muster Verb + Partikel + Objekt oder Verb + Objekt + Partikel ausgedrückt werden:
I need to look up this word. = I need to look this word up.
Nadeem wants to ask out Sophie. = Nadeem wants to ask Sophie out.

Wenn das Objekt ein Personalpronomen ist, muss der Satz dem Muster Verb + Objekt + Partikel folgen:
I need to look it up. (~~I need to look up it.~~)

Übung 14: **Wählen Sie die richtige Form.**

1. Please fill ______________ *(ausfüllen)* this form.
a) in b) up c) over
2. I would like to try it ______________ *(ausprobieren)*.
a) out b) up c) over
3. Would you like to try ______________ *(anprobieren)* this blouse?
a) over b) in c) on

Verben *have, take, make, do*

Es gibt im Englischen viele feste Ausdrücke, bei denen diese Verben gebraucht werden, wie z.B.:

have	breakfast, a cup of tea, a conversation, a shower (GB)
take	a shower (USA), a holiday, a break, a decision (GB)
make	a date, friends, dinner, a decision (USA)
do	the housework, the shopping

Im Gebrauch von *do* und *make* gibt es Unterschiede zwischen dem Deutschen und dem Englischen: Im Englischen verwendet man *do* im Zusammenhang mit Tätigkeiten, Arbeit und Reaktionen.
I should **do** my homework. (Ich sollte meine Hausaufgaben **machen**.)

Man verwendet *make*, wenn etwas hergestellt wird, auch wenn das Objekt abstrakt ist:
I **make** breakfast for the family every morning.

Übung 15: **Ergänzen Sie die Sätze mit *have, take, make* oder *do*.**

1. She must ______________ a difficult decision.
2. I ______________ a shower after I work out.
3. He likes to ______________ a drink with friends after work.
4. We need to ______________ our homework before tomorrow.
5. They are ______________ a holiday in the Lake District this autumn.

6 London calling

Wortschatz	Kommunikation	Grammatik
Stadtverkehr Orientierung und Richtung	Nach dem Weg fragen Wege beschreiben Über Vergangenes sprechen	Simple Past (Präteritum)

Excuse me, I'm having a little trouble and I don't know how to get to Morton's Tower.
No problem. First you take the Victoria line to Oxford Circus. From there...
...take the Bakerloo Line to Lambeth North.
1
2
3
4
5
Then, take the bus to Lambeth Palace.

Excuse me. I was looking for a café near the Tower...
Say what now? A flower café? What on earth is that?
No, no. A café near Morton Tower. The Garden Café.
Ah yes... Well, you walk down this road, and it should be on the left side.
Thank you!
These young folks... Always in a hurry...
Where could he be? I hope he didn't forget...
There you are, Nadeem!
Sophie, I'm so sorry I'm late... I... um... I just need to catch my breath.

This place is lovely. What's the name of this road?
It's called The Queen's Walk. It's one of my favorite places. I came here a lot when I was younger.
That thing looks massive!
Wait till you have a look from the top. The view is one of the best in London.
I remember you said you didn't like heights. How are you feeling, Nadeem?
Don't worry, Sophie. Your idea was the best. I feel great. Actually,
I've never felt better.

Wortschatz

Stadtverkehr

crossroad(s)

roundabout

bridge

parking space

zebra crossing

river

pedestrian zone

traffic light(s)

tunnel

marketplace

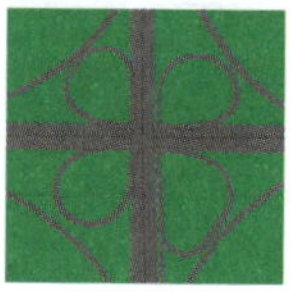
motorway

Übung 1: **Was ist X? Ergänzen Sie das Wort.**

a) We can get there faster if we take the **X** and not the city roads. ______________________

b) People go on foot in the **X**. There are no cars here. ______________________

c) I don't like driving in the city. You never find a **X**. ______________________

d) The **X** is red. Pedestrians and drivers have to wait. ______________________

e) Pedestrians can cross the street by using a **X**. Cars must wait. ______________________

f) A car is driving over the **X**. ______________________

In vielen Straßennamen in Großbritannien finden sich folgende Wörter:

street/road (Straße)
way (Hauptstraße)
avenue (ursprünglich „Allee", aber jetzt einfach eine Wohnstraße)
drive (Wohnstraße)
lane (Gasse, Wohnstraße)
place (Platz)

Orientierung und Richtung

Mit dem Auto, zu Fuß:

1

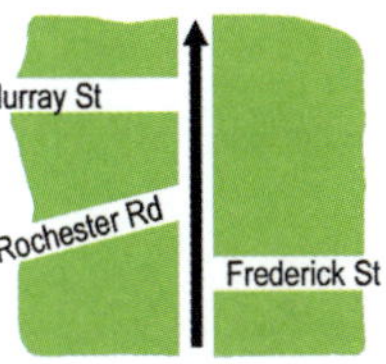

2

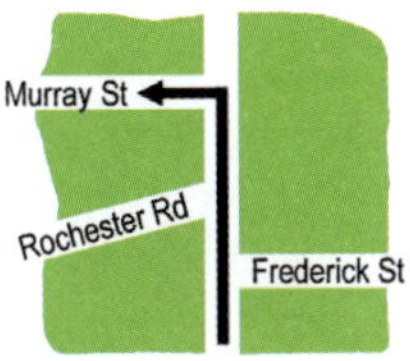

3

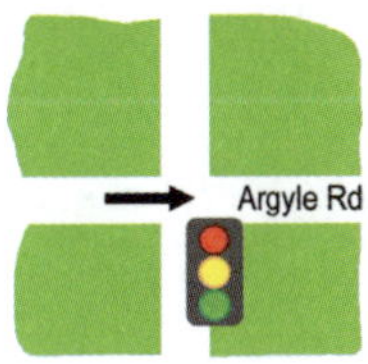

4

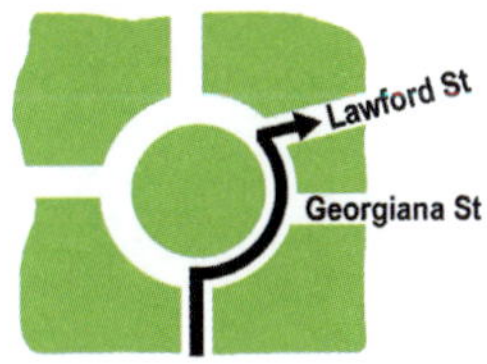

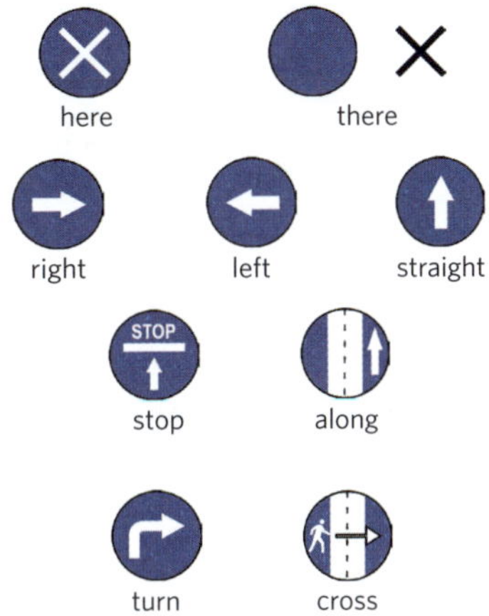

Übung 2: **Zu welchem Bild passt die Beschreibung? Kreuzen Sie an.**

	1	2	3	4
a) go over the crossroad(s)	☐	☐	☐	☐
b) go straight	☐	☐	☐	☐
c) turn left	☐	☐	☐	☐
d) go all the way to the roundabout, take the second street on the right	☐	☐	☐	☐
e) go along this street	☐	☐	☐	☐

Mit der U-Bahn, mit dem Bus:

Where do I need to **get on**?
On/at platform 3.

Do I need to change trains?
No, it's a direct line. /Yes, at Holborn station.

Where do I get off?
At "Holland Park".

Kommunikation

Nach dem Weg fragen – Wege beschreiben

Excuse me, where is | how do I get to ...?
I'm looking for a post office | the train station | Oxford Rd.

Go straight | to the right | to the left.
Go all the way to the crossroad(s) | the traffic light(s).
Then take the first | second street on the right-hand side | left-hand side.
There you'll see ...

Thanks! | Thank you very much!

You're welcome!/That's okay

Übung 3: **Lesen Sie die Wegbeschreibung. Wohin möchte die Person?**

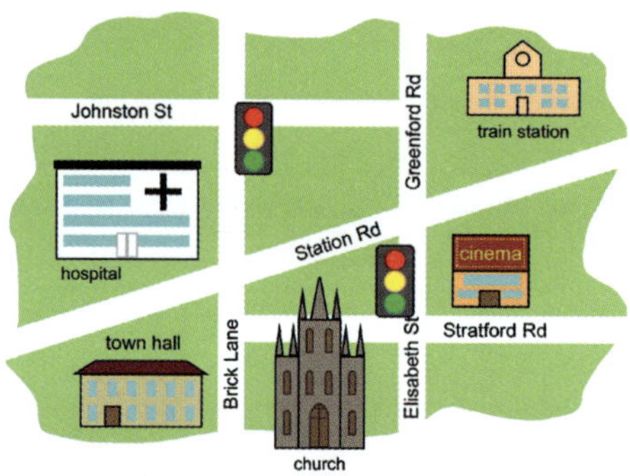

How do I get from the church to the ____________________?

Turn right onto Brick Lane and continue straight until you see the traffic light. At the light turn right onto Johnston St and go straight. Then, turn right onto Greenford Rd and go straight until you see Station Rd. Turn left onto Station Rd and the ________________ will be on your left.

Übung 4: **Beschreiben Sie den Weg.**

a) How do I get to the cinema from the station? ______________________________

____

____

b) How do I get from the town hall to Greenford Rd? ______________________________

____

____

Über Vergangenes sprechen

Übung 5: Und gestern? Ordnen Sie die Sätze zu.

What are you doing today?

a) I'm getting up later than usual.

b) I'm showering in my new bathroom.

c) I'm making breakfast for Mary.

d) I'm going to work in the London office.

e) I'm calling customers from home.

f) I'm having lunch with my boss.

g) I'm coming home early.

What did you do yesterday?

___ A I ate lunch with my boss.

___ B I called customers from home.

___ C I made breakfast for Mary.

___ D I showered in my new bathroom.

___ E I went to work in the London office.

___ F I got up later than usual.

___ G I came home early.

Übung 6: Was hat Nadeem gemacht? Schreiben Sie Sätze im Simple Past:

arrive at the café | ask a man for directions | enjoy the view from the top |
ride the bus | speak with an elderly woman | take the tube | visit the London Eye

1 ____________________

2 ____________________

3 ____________________

4 ____________________

5 ____________________

6 ____________________

7 ____________________

Grammatik

Simple Past (Präteritum)

Man benutzt im Englischen das Simple Past, um abgeschlossene Handlungen aus der aktuellen oder ferneren Vergangenheit auszudrücken. Im Gegensatz zum deutschen Präteritum wird das Simple Past häufig auch in der gesprochenen Sprache verwendet:

I visited my grandmother this weekend.
The orchestra played for two hours.
He travelled to London for two weeks.
She carried the groceries home.

Bei regelmäßigen Verben, **die nicht auf -e oder -y enden**, bildet man das Simple Past mit der Grundform des Verbes + -ed:	learn → learned
Wenn die Grundform des Verbes **mit einem Vokal und einem Konsonant endet**, muss der Konsonant häufig gedoppelt werden:	stop → stopped
Bei regelmäßigen Verben, **die mit -e enden**, bildet man das Simple Past mit der Grundform des Verbes + -d:	live → lived dance → danced
Bei regelmäßigen Verben, **die mit einem Konsonant und -y enden**, bildet man das Simple Past mit der Grundform des Verbes + -ied	carry → carried worry → worried
Bei regelmäßigen Verben, die **mit einem Vokal und -y enden**, bildet man das Simple Past with der Grundform des Verbes + -ed	stay → stayed

Übung 7: **Formulieren Sie die Sätze in Sätze mit dem Simple Past um.**

1. She walks to school. ______________________________
2. He calls his friends on the phone. ______________________________
3. We want to go on holiday. ______________________________
4. They live in Leicester. ______________________________
5. I prefer cake over chips. ______________________________
6. You worry about me. ______________________________

Es gibt aber viele unregelmäßige Verben im Englischen, deren Simple-Past-Formen auswendig gelernt werden müssen. Eine Tabelle der wichtigsten Verben finden Sie im Anhang.

Das Verb *to be* ist das einzige Verb, dessen Simple-Past-Form nicht bei allen Formen gleich ist:

I was	we were
you were	you were
he/she/it was	they were

Übung 8: Schreiben Sie das Verb in Klammern im Simple Past.

1. I *(forget)* ______________ my friend's birthday yesterday!
2. We *(see)* ______________ a good movie/film at the weekend.
3. The kids *(get)* __________ lots of presents at/for Christmas.
4. He *(write)* ___________ a letter to his favorite author.
5. They *(teach)* ______________ French for 40 years.
6. We *(eat)* ______________ too much at the party.
7. The concert *(be)* ____________ lovely.
8. The guests *(be)* ______________ interesting.
9. They *(go)* ______________ to the Canary Islands last summer.
10. I *(can)* ______________ play the violin when I *(be)* _____________ a child.

Übung 9: Erzählen Sie davon, was Sie letztes Jahr im Urlaub gemacht haben.

Last year on holiday I ... ____

____

____

____

Verneinte Aussagen im Simple Past bildet man mit **did not (didn't) + der Grundform des Verbs**:
I'm sorry, but I didn't understand you.
We didn't go out to dinner last night.
He didn't take the bus to work yesterday.

Übung 10: Bilden Sie verneinte Sätze.

1. We went to school on foot. ______________________________________
2. They sang traditional songs. ____________________________________
3. The meal cost a lot. ____
4. The group chose a fascinating book. ______________________________
5. I thought so. _______________________________________
6. She sent the package on time. _________________________________

Fragen im Simple Past bildet man mit **did/didn't + Subjekt + Grundform des Verbs**:
Did they have a nice time?
Didn't you like it?
Where did you go?
Who did you see?

Die einzige Ausnahme ist das Verb to be. Man bildet Fragen mit to be mit **was/were** oder **wasn't/weren't**:
Was the play good?
Weren't they great!
Where were you?

7

My home is my castle

Wortschatz	Kommunikation	Grammatik
Haus, Wohnung, Zimmer Wohnungseinrichtung Tätigkeiten im Haushalt	Eine Wohnung finden und beschreiben	Präpositionen Present Perfect Contractions

We don't have much time... Could you wash the dishes while I clean my bedroom?
?
I'm taking out the trash. Could you put these clothes in the washing machine?
Oh, by the way, the vacuum cleaner is in the closet in the hallway. Would you please vacuum the living room and the kitchen?
Should I light candles?
Sophie, you are killing me...

So far, so good. We still have some work to do before Nadeem arrives.
Could you put these books on the shelf, please?
Could you bring these magazines down into the basement?
Do you collect all this junk?
...clean the mirror
And if you have some energy left, please clean the dresser, too.
Thanks for your help!
Not a problem! Have fun with Romeo!

DING, DONG
Hello Sophie. These are for you.
Aaw...They are lovely. Please, come inside.
You can hang up your coat on the coat rack.
Let me give you a tour of my little home... This is the living room.
My bedroom...
And my kitchen, of course.

Dinner is served, hope you like it.
Looks great, Sophie. Hope you didn't go to too much trouble because of me.
Nonsense, I like to cook. Would you like to have a glass of water?
Yes, that would be lovely.
Thank you for the meal, it tasted great! Say, have you ever been to the States?
No, but I have always wanted to go there. I just love to travel when I have the time.
How many countries have you been to?
I have been to New Zealand, Greece, France and Singapore. Japan and Cuba are on my list for the future. And America, of course.
That sounds exciting! I've never been anywhere in Asia before. What about your hobbies?
I have been taking classes in photography. I enjoy taking pictures during my travels or when I go for a walk.
Later that evening...
Can I see you tomorrow?
I'd like that... I'll call you in the morning.

Wortschatz

Haus – Wohnung – Zimmer

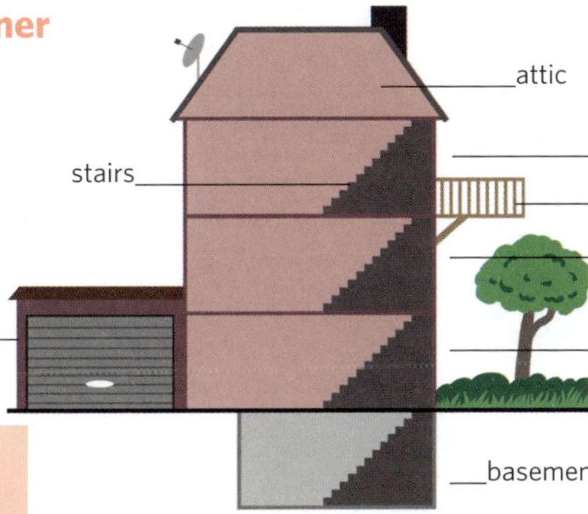

> ! 🇺🇸 ground floor = first floor
> first floor = second floor
> second floor = third floor usw.

Übung 1: **Wie wohnen Sie? Schreiben Sie Antworten in ganzen Sätzen.**

a) Which floor do you live on? *I live on the* ______________________________.

b) How many rooms does your apartment / house have? ______________________________.

c) Does your apartment | house have a balcony? ______________________________.

d) Do you also have a garden | a garage | a basement/cellar? ______________________________.

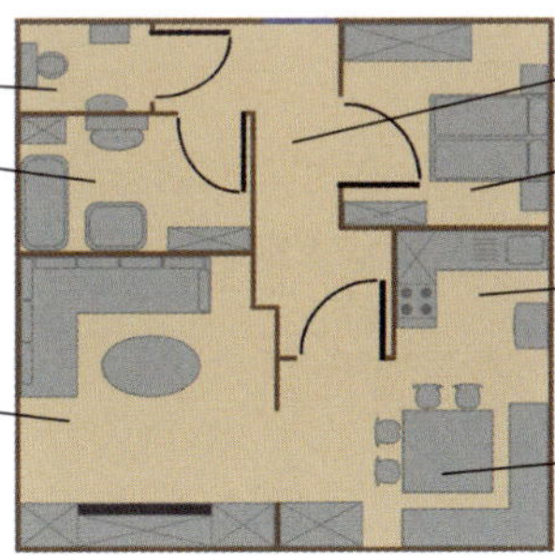

Übung 2: **Wie heißt das Zimmer?**

a) This is where you watch TV: ______________________________

b) This is where you have a shower or bath: ______________________________

c) This is where you cook: ______________________________

d) This is where you sleep: ______________________________

e) This is where you have a meal: ______________________________

Wohnungseinrichtung

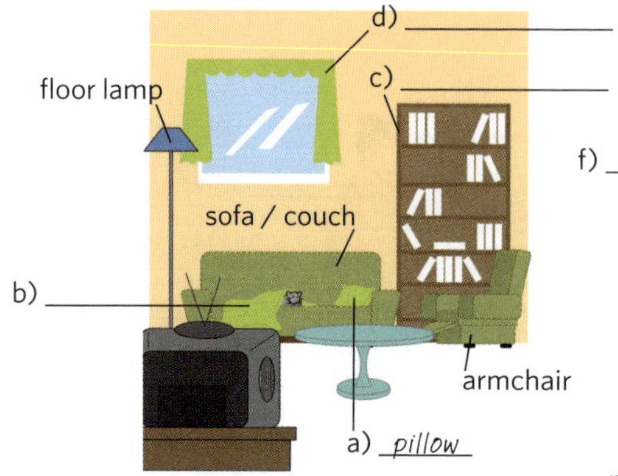

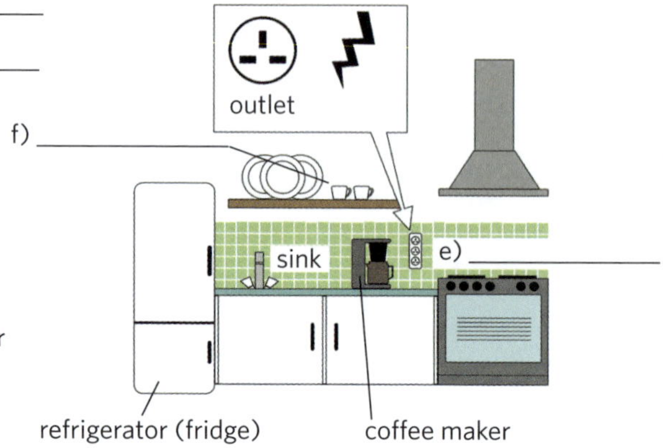

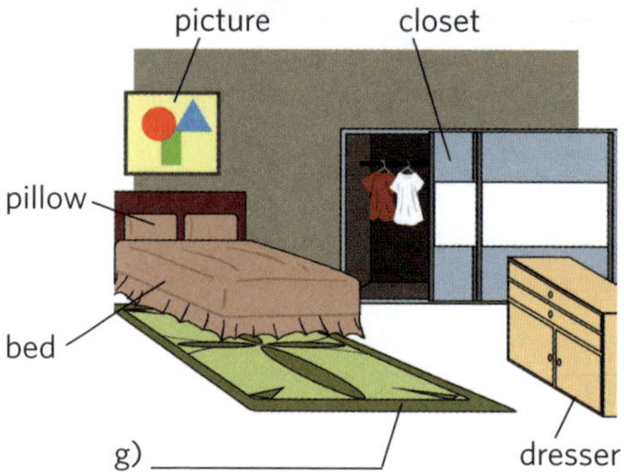

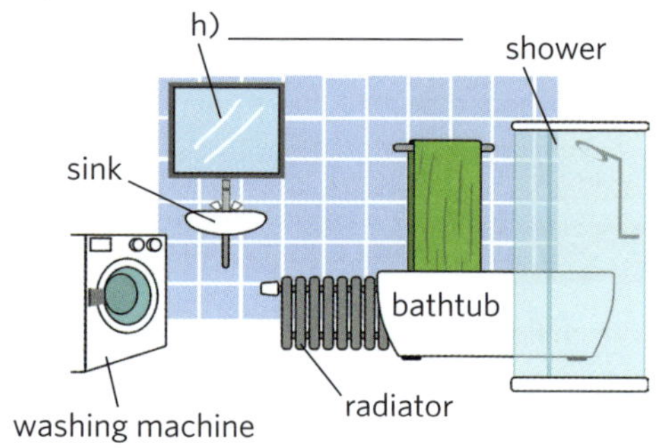

Übung 3: **Lesen Sie die Sätze und schreiben Sie die markierten Möbelstücke und Gegenstände zu den Zeichnungen a) bis h).**

There is a mirror hanging over the sink.
You can cook on the stove.
There are many books on the shelf.
There's a yellow pillow and a blanket on the sofa.
Here are the dishes and the coffee maker.
There's a rug under the bed.
There's a curtain hanging in front of the window.

Tätigkeiten im Haushalt

dirty clean

to clean

messy tidy

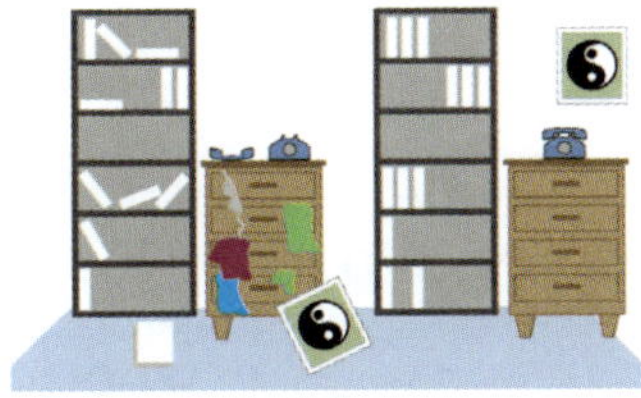

to tidy up

to throw away

to iron

the laundry

to water

Übung 4: Sauber und ordentlich! Welches Verb passt?

a) shirts and trousers
b) cats and dogs
c) windows, the kitchen, the bathroom, the cellar
d) old newspapers
e) dirty clothes, laundry
f) the carpet, rugs
g) flowers, plants, the garden
h) the bedroom, the living room

___ A throw away
___ B water
___ C tidy up
___ D clean
___ E hoover/vacuum
___ F iron
___ G feed
___ H wash

Übung 5: Beschreiben Sie Ihr Traumhaus!

My dream house has ______________________________

____

______________________________.

Kommunikation

Wohnung gefunden!

Room to Let
Attic room, 15 sqm, kitchen, bathroom
only 10 minutes away from the University; Tube stop nearby
500 £, all inclusive
Phone: (0)20 4600 5400

Übung 6: **Studentin Emily erzählt einer Freundin von ihrer neuen Wohnung. Ordnen Sie den Dialog.**

___ a) 15 square metres. I can make do with that.
___ b) 500 £, all inclusive.
___ c) That's brilliant! How many rooms has it got?
___ d) On Saturday. You can come and help, if you'd like. The address is...
___ e) 500 £ is good for London. When do you move in?
___ f) It's a bit small, isn't it? How big is the room?
___ g) I've finally found a flat!
___ h) Yes, that's pretty big. How much is the rent?
___ i) Just the one. There's also a small kitchen and bath.

Übung 7: **Getrennt durch eine gemeinsame Sprache. Was würde Sophie sagen und was würde Nadeem sagen? Ordnen Sie die britischen Wörter ihren US-amerikanischen Äquivalenten zu.**

a) flat	___ A cookies
b) underground	___ B apartment
c) holiday (Urlaub)	___ C vacation
d) autumn	___ D sneakers
e) lift	___ E subway
f) sweets (Süßigkeiten)	___ F fall
g) crisps	___ G elevator
h) trainers (Turnschuhe)	___ H candy
i) biscuits (Kekse)	___ I to stand in line
j) to queue	___ J chips

Grammatik

Präpositionen

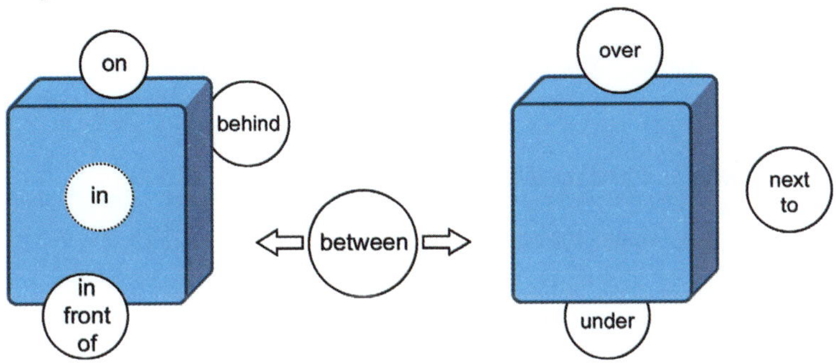

Übung 8: Wo sind die Mäuse? Ergänzen Sie:

on | behind | in | next to (x2) | under | in front of | between

a) Dennis is sitting ____________ the sofa, ____________ Olivia.

b) Oscar is sitting ____________ the sofa, ____________ the cushions.

c) Andy is standing ____________ the sofa.

d) Ben is lying ____________ the sofa.

e) Paul is lying ____________ the sofa.

f) Gunther is ____________ the sofa.

Present Perfect

Das Present Perfect im Englischen bezieht sich auf ein Geschehnis in der Vergangenheit, das eine Wirkung auf die Gegenwart hat. Es wird im Normalfall mit dem Hilfsverb to have + Partizip (Grundform des Verbs + (e)d/ied) gebildet.
We have never visited London.
Their son has recently started his studies at Oxford.

Das Hilfsverb wird häufig von Adverbien wie **ever** (je), **never** (nie), **recently** (vor kurzem) und **already** (schon) gefolgt. **Yet** (schon) kommt immer am Ende des Satzes.

Übung 9: Bilden Sie das Partizip der Verben in Klammern.

1. Have you ________________ (wash) the car yet?
2. I have already ________________ (complete) my homework for next week.
3. My grandparents have never ________________ (talk) with us over Skype before.
4. They have recently ________________ (move) to this address.
5. Have you ever ________________ (live) abroad?

Es gibt aber viele irreguläre Partizipien, die auswendig gelernt müssen. Die wichtigsten finden Sie in der Tabelle im Anhang.

Übung 10: Ergänzen Sie mit einem unregelmäßigen Partizip.

1. The Tigers have recently ________________ (win) the state championship.
2. Have you ________________ (fed) the cat yet today?
3. Sophie has never ________________ (sing) before a crowd.
4. The lawyer has already ________________ (write) the contract.
5. Have you ever ________________ (eat) Haggis?
6. Nadeem has never ________________ (see) anyone as lovely as Sophie.
7. I have never ________________ (sleep) in past noon.
8. Have you already ________________ (speak) to her about the party?
9. We have ________________ (know) them for five years.
10. Claire has recently ________________ (begin) piano lessons.

Übung 11: **Simple Past oder Present Perfect? Übersetzen Sie ins Englische.**

1. Ich habe noch nie etwas Leckereres gegessen!

   ____!

2. Am Wochenende sind wir ins Kino gegangen.

   ____.

3. Wir sind schon oft in dieses Restaurant gegangen.

   ____.

4. Ich habe sie neulich gesehen.

   ____.

5. Letzten Sommer haben wir Urlaub auf Kreta gemacht.

   ____.

Contractions im Englischen

Wie Sie in den vorherigen Lektionen gesehen haben, gibt es im Englischen viele Subjekt-Verb-Kombinationen , die man mithilfe eines Apostrophs verkürzen kann. Man nennt das contraction, also Zusammenziehung. Dies gilt auch für das Present Perfect:

I've (= I have) never seen her before.

She's (= she has) recently been to Ireland.

Übung 12: **Ergänzen Sie folgende Tabelle mit den richtigen contractions.**

are not	*aren't*	we are	*we're*
can not		they are	
could not		she has	
do not		I have	
should not		we have	
were not		they have	
will not		he will	
it is		I will	
he is		we will	
I am		they will	

8 Love hurts!

Wortschatz	Kommunikation	Grammatik
Lebensmittel Menge, Gewicht, Verpackung Körperteile	Krankheit und Gesundheit Medikamente Beim Arzt Auf dem Markt	Imperativ *Much/many* und *little/few*

Later...
Good morning you two, what can I do for you?
Hello, I'd like five apples, one pound of cherries and a pound of strawberries.
Here you are, anything else?
We need a head of lettuce, too
One fresh lettuce it shall be. That's 3.10₺ all together.
We should see the butcher, too.
One pound of minced meat and six slices of turkey, please. How much does that come to?
Let's see... mince... turkey... 5.80₺, love.

Alright, we still need milk, cream, cheese and lasagna sheets. The supermarket is that way.
Nadeem!
AH!
What happened?
I tripped and twisted my ankle... Just my luck...
Does it hurt bad?
It's nothing, I can manage... Where was the supermarket again?
Nonsense, you can't walk around like that! You need a doctor.
mumble...
TAXI!

Mr Khan, please?
...So I was walking through the market place and suddenly twisted my ankle... It's nothing really...
Hm, I don't know... Looks badly injured... We might have to consider an amputation...
AMPUTATION?!
Relax, I was just kidding... It's just a little sprained. Rest your leg for a few days and you're good as new.
Dear God...
You can call me Doc. I'll give you a prescription for an ointment that will ease the pain.
Take care, Mr Khan!

Wortschatz

Lebensmittel

Übung 1: **Ein Wort passt nicht in die Reihe. Kreuzen Sie an.**

a) fruit:	☐ lemons	☐ potatoes	☐ strawberries	☐ apples
b) vegetables:	☐ tomatoes	☐ onions	☐ noodles	☐ cucumbers
c) dairy products:	☐ yoghurt	☐ lettuce	☐ butter	☐ cheese
d) meat:	☐ chicken	☐ ham	☐ turkey	☐ fish
e) drinks and beverages:	☐ beer	☐ milk	☐ rice	☐ wine

Übung 2: **Wo kauft man ...? Ergänzen Sie:**

bakery | butcher's | market | supermarket | drink shop

You can buy baked goods at the ____________________, meat at the ____________________, and fruit and vegetables at the ____________________. Of course, you can also get all of these items at the ____________________. In some states in the US, you have to buy alcoholic beverages at a ____________________.

Menge – Gewicht – Verpackung

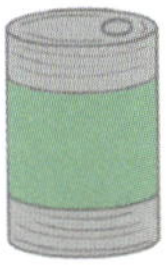
can

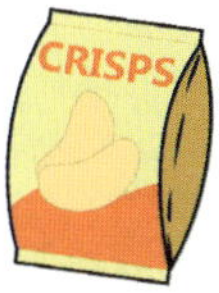

bag

bottle

litre

box

jar

package

pound

> ! The popular dessert pound cake gets its name from its original recipe, which called for one pound each of sugar, eggs, flour, and butter.

Übung 3: **Was steht auf der Einkaufsliste? Ergänzen Sie mit den richtigen Zutaten.**

a) a ________________ of jam
b) a ________________ of beans
c) a ________________ of noodles
d) a ________________ of water
e) a ________________ of olive oil
f) a ________________ of sweets
g) a ________________ of rice

Übung 4: **Welche Zutaten brauchen Sie für Ihr Lieblingsgericht? Schreiben Sie in ganzen Sätzen.**

____
____
____
____
____

Körperteile

Der Körper:

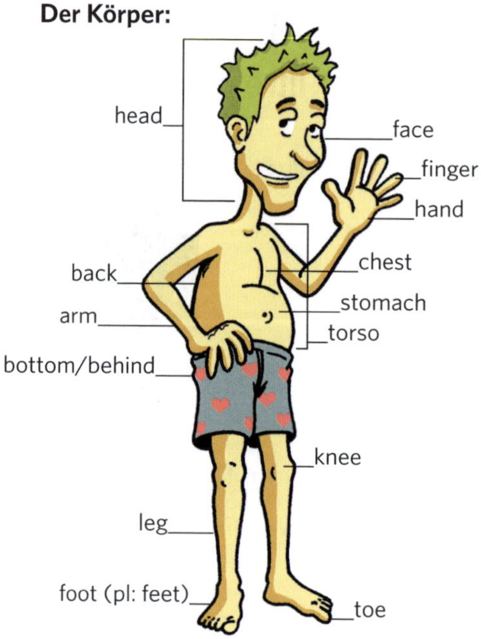

Das Gesicht:

Übung 5: **Welcher Körperteil ist das? Schreiben Sie die Wörter.**

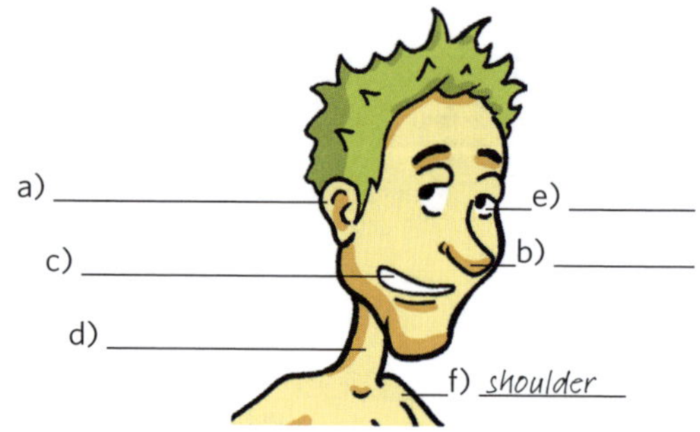

~~shoulder~~ | mouth | eye | ear | neck | nose

Übung 6: **Wie heißt der Körperteil in den folgenden englischen Ausdrücken? Ergänzen Sie.**

back
chest
feet
hands
knees
stomach
head

a) "Cold ________________, warm heart." (Nutzt man, wenn man die Hände von jemandem schüttelt, die besonders kalt sind.)

b) "My eyes were bigger than my ____________________." (Auf Deutsch: Meine Augen waren größer als der Magen.)

c) "Don't worry! I've got your __________________." (Nutzt man, wenn man jemanden unterstützt.)

d) -"Ms Smith's class never has that many people in it."
-"Well, she's not very good. The students vote with their _______________."
(Auf Deutsch: mit den Füßen abstimmen)

e) "Honey, can I speak to you in private? I need to get something off my _________________."
(Nutzt man, wenn einen etwas beschäftigt, das man unbedingt besprechen muss.)

f) "Use your _______________!" (Auf Deutsch: Benutze deinen Kopf!)

g) When Nadeem sees Sophie, he gets weak in the _________________. (Nutzt man, um Verliebtheit zubeschreiben.)

Übung 7: **Von Kopf bis Fuß. Ordnen Sie die Körperteile von oben nach unten.**

____ two feet, ____ two shoulders, ____ two legs, ____two hands, ____ two eyes, ____ two arms, ____ two knees

Kommunikation

Krankheit und Gesundheit

Übung 8: **Was fehlt diesen Personen? Zu jedem Bild passen zwei Sätze. Ordnen Sie zu.**

a) I have a cold.
b) I have a stomachache.
c) I have a backache.
d) I feel nauseous.
e) I can't stand up straight.
f) I have a fever and a headache.

Übung 9: **Geben Sie den Personen aus Übung 8 einen Gesundheitstipp. Ordnen Sie die Bilder zu. Manchmal passen zwei Bilder.**

a) Work less! Do sport!	Picture ___
b) Take an aspirin and drink some tea!	Picture ___
c) Go to the chemist's and get a pain relief cream!	Picture ___
d) Take a break from working out for a bit!	Picture ___

Medikamente

cough syrup

pill

ointment

Beim Arzt

Im Sprechzimmer

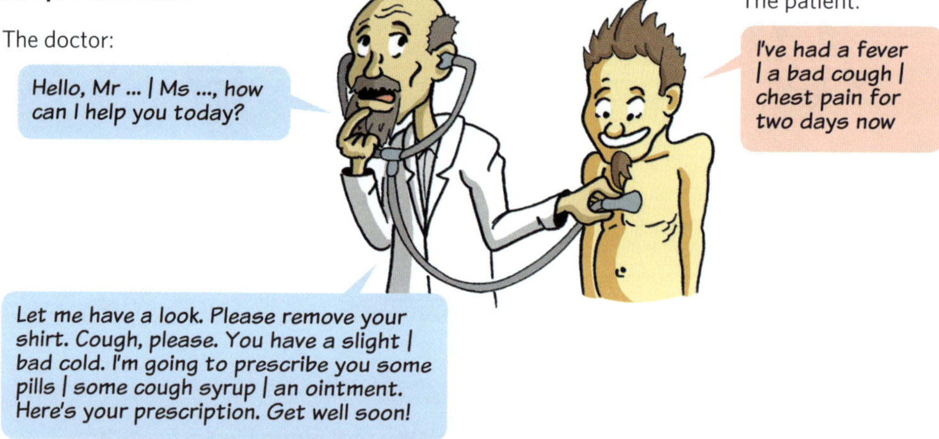

Übung 10: **Sie sind krank und wollen zum Arzt gehen. Was machen Sie zuerst? Und dann? Nummerieren Sie.**

___ a) The doctor prescribes medication.
___ b) You have a seat in the waiting room.
___ c) You call the office and make an appointment.
___ d) You take the medication at home.
___ e) The doctor speaks with you and examines you.
___ f) The receptionist calls you to the consultation room.
___ g) You go to the doctor's office, sign in at the front desk, and give your insurance card to the receptionist.
___ h) You take your prescription to the chemist's and pick up your medication there.

Auf dem Markt

Who's next in line? What can I get you?

I'd like ...

How much does a pound of ________ cost?
What's the price of the ___________?

They cost | They're ________ a pound.

What else can I get you?

I'd also like ...
That's all, thanks. How much does it come to?

That comes to _____________ in total.

Übung 11: **In der Eisdiele. Ordnen Sie den Dialog.**

___ a) Hello! Who's next in line?
___ b) Here you are and keep the change!
___ c) Her big sister can help if needed. How much does that come to?
___ d) We are! I'd like a cone with a scoop of mint chocolate chip and a scoop of bourbon vanilla, please, and my little sister would like a hot fudge sundae. How much is it with whipped cream and sprinkles?
___ e) The cone and sundae together come to 7.80 £ in total.
___ f) Thanks and have a great day!
___ g) It's 5.50 £. But are you sure her eyes aren't bigger than her stomach?

Grammatik

Imperativ

Die Bildung des Imperativs im Englischen ist erfrischend einfach: Für alle Formen braucht man nur die Infinitivform des Verbs (natürlich ohne das „to") zu verwenden:

Get up! It's already 11 a.m.!

Make sure to pick up milk on the way home, please.

Add red pepper to the sauce to make it spicy.

Bei negativen Ausdrücken fügt man „don't" vor dem Verb ein:

Don't forget to call mum!

Don't lose track of time!

Für Vorschläge nutzt man „let's" (= let us):

Let's go to the movies this weekend!

But I'm not sure if we'll have time. Let's wait and see.

Für negative Vorschläge fügt man ein „not" nach dem „let's" ein:

Let's not wait another minute!

> Sprachwitz: What did the vegetable pastor say to the vegetable church? Lettuce pray!

Übung 12: **Nadeem und Sophie machen zusammen eine Lasagne. Ergänzen Sie das Rezept mit den richtigen Verben.**

bake | cook | fry | layer *(schichten)* | mix | simmer *(köcheln)* | stir *(rühren)*

____________ the noodles according to the directions on the package.

____________ the minced meat with onion and garlic until brown in oil.

____________ in the tomatoes, tomato paste, water, sugar, pepper, salt, and herbs.

____________ for 30 minutes.

____________ egg and ricotta cheese in a bowl.

____________ the noodles, beef, and cheese mixture in a casserole dish.

____________ for 25 minutes in the oven.

Übung 13: **Übersetzen Sie ins Englische.**

a) Trink mehr Tee! ______________________________

b) Essen Sie mehr Obst! ______________________________

c) Sei um 14 Uhr da! ______________________________

d) Seien Sie nicht zu spät! ______________________________

Den Imperativ kann man natürlich mit dem Wort „please" höflicher formulieren, aber das Englische hat eine Vorliebe für indirekte Fragen, besonders in der Öffentlichkeit, im professionellen Kontext und unter Menschen, die mit einander weniger bekannt sind. (Auch Freunde und Familienmitglieder nutzen indirekte Fragen untereinander für einen freundlicheren Umgang.) Diese Fragen nutzen W-Fragewörter sowie „if" *(ob)*.

I'm not sure how to get to the doctor's office.
I have no idea how much this costs.
I didn't understand what you said.
I was wondering if we could go to the movies this weekend.
She would like to know if we are planning to come to her birthday party.

Much/many und little/few

Im Wortschatzteil haben Sie sich mit einigen zählbaren (wie *eggs* und *carrots*) und unzählbaren (wie *bread*, *rice* und *milk*) Nomen vertraut gemacht. Hier sind wichtige Nomen, die im Englischen unzählbar, im Deutschen hingegen zählbar sind:

advice (Ratschläge)
My mother gives great advice (nicht ~~great advices~~)

homework (Hausaufgaben)
We have a lot of homework this weekend. (nicht ~~a lot of homeworks~~)

information (Infos)
Thank you very kindly for the information! (nicht ~~for the informations~~)

Much (viel) und **little** (wenig) nutzt man mit unzählbaren Nomen, **many** (viele) und **few** (wenige) nutzt man mit zählbaren Nomen:

There is much to see in London!
I have little hope (Hoffnung) that he'll come. (hope = unzählbar)
There were so many people at the concert! (people = zählbar)
He has few friends. (friends = zählbar)

Da **little** und **few** schon Negativität ausdrücken, muss man in Sätzen mit dem Wort **not much** und **many** verwenden:

It doesn't cost much money.
He doesn't have many friends.

Übung 14: **Ergänzen Sie mit much/many oder little/few.**

a) I'm sorry, but I can't go Sunday night. I have so ____________ homework to do!

b) She's new to the city and she doesn't know ______________ people here yet.

c) It can be hard to find an affordable place to stay the night in London. There are ____________ cheap hotels.

d) Hurry up! We have ____________ time to waste!

e) This recipe is great! It takes 20 minutes and you need __________ ingredients *(Zutaten)* to make it.

9 Meet the parents

Wortschatz	Kommunikation	Grammatik
Berufe Schulfächer	Über Schule und Ausbildung sprechen Im Restaurant	Futur – *will, going to* und *present progressive* Nebensätze Gerundium oder Infinitiv?

The next day...
What's wrong Nadeem? You've been awfully quiet since we left. Are you OK?
Oh, it's about your parents... Don't you think it's a little early for me to meet them?
You're just nervous, that's all. Don't worry, they won't eat you.
I've told them all about you, and they're really looking forward to meet you. Everything will be just fine, trust me.
If you say so, Sophie.

Here we are. Are you ready?
Do I have a choice?
Hi Mum, this is Nadeem.
Hello, Mrs Robinson. Pleasure to meet you.
The pleasure is all mine, Nadeem. We've heard all about you! I'm Nancy. Come on in, my husband is in the kitchen.
Here, I have a little something for you...
Oh, you shouldn't have! Chocolate is my weak spot, ha ha.

Hi, Dad, this is Nadeem.
Oh, hello there young man! I'm afraid that I'm still a bit busy preparing dinner. Hope you like fish. Please, have a seat in the dining room and make yourself comfortable.

Sophie has told us that you work for a textile company in the States, is that correct?
Yes. When I finished studying marketing and sales, I started working for Great Lakes. Now I'm a sales manager and am in charge of international projects and customers.
That's impressive! My wife and I were wondering where you were originally from.
My parents are from Pakistan, but I was born in the States.
Interesting. Quite an adventurous life you have there, don't you agree, Nancy?
Oh yes, I'd like to hear more about it.

Honey, Nadeem is really nice, but the long distance concerns me. How will you two maintain a relationship if...
Relax mom, we're taking it slow. I'm going to visit him in Chicago! We'll spend two weeks together. I'll meet his family, and maybe we'll even go on a little road trip together.
Ah, I think you just gave me an idea...
My wife works part time at the post office, while I've been working as an optician.
How long have you been working in that field?
For over twenty years now. I opened my own shop outside of London ten years ago. But I think I'm going to retire in about eight years. I'd like to see a bit of the world while I'm still young, you know?

Later that day...
So which airline would you recommend for us? I mean all of us.
You'll see, we'll have a splendid time together.
WHAT?!
Look, they're offering great trips around Manhattan and the Statue of Liberty. Free drinks and a baseball cap.
USA
...And I've always wanted to see Washington, and Florida, too. Oh, and the Hollywood Walk of Fame! You must take us there!
...um...
Maybe business class could be arranged, what do you think Nadeem? Surely you have connections and frequent flyer miles, right? What do you think, Sophie? Sophie??
And which airline did you say that we should take? Is it better to sit in window or aisle seats? Nadeem?

Wortschatz

Berufe

salesperson

bank clerk

hairdresser | hair stylist

veterinarian

journalist

scientist

mechanic

carpenter

teacher

Übung 1: **Wer sagt das? Ergänzen Sie den Beruf.**

a) ______________________: I write articles for a newspaper.
b) ______________________: I cut and style hair at a salon.
c) ______________________: I work on a construction team and build houses.
d) ______________________: I teach mathematics at a school.
e) ______________________: I help sick animals.
f) ______________________: I sell products at a department store.
g) ______________________: I develop experiments in my laboratory.
h) ______________________: I repair cars in a garage.
i) ______________________: I studied finance.

Das Wort *apprenticeship* (Ausbildung) nutzt man nur im Rahmen von Berufen, die man als *trades* (Handwerk, Gewerbe) bezeichnen würde. Formelle Ausbildungen für Berufe wie Kellner und Bankkauffrau kennen die anglophonen Länder nicht. In nicht handwerklichen Berufsfeldern spricht man von *internships* (Praktika), *traineeships*, oder *on-the-job training*.

Anders als in Deutschland mit seinen drei verschiedenen Schulformen gibt es im Vereinigten Königreich die *senior school* nach der *elementary school* (Grundschule) und in den USA die *high school*. Im Alter von 15 oder 16 schreibt man im Vereinigten Königreich das GCSE-Examen *(General Certificate of Secondary Education)* und geht danach zur *sixth form* oder ins *college*, wo man nach zwei Jahren seine A-levels (Abitur) macht, auf eine *vocational school* (Berufschule), um einem Gewerbe nachzugehen, oder fängt gleich an zu arbeiten. In den USA machen alle das *high school diploma* und gehen danach entweder direkt auf die Universität, zu einer Berufsschule oder auf den freien Markt.

Schulfächer

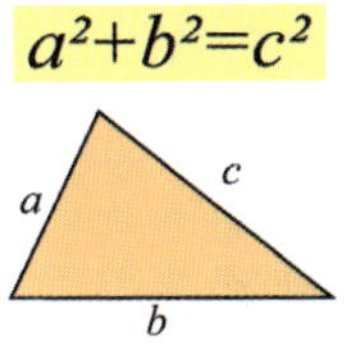

maths (US: math)

art

chemistry

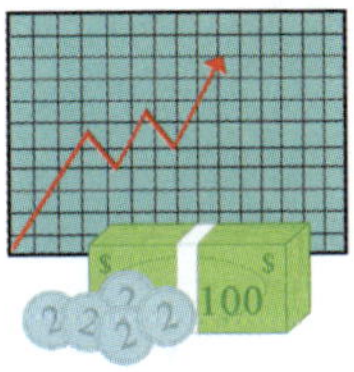

economics

physics

religion

geography

English

history

Übung 2: **In welchen Fächern lernt man etwas über folgende Persönlichkeiten? Ergänzen Sie mit Fächern aus der Tabelle.**

a) Andy Warhol ____________________

b) Magellan ____________________

c) Jane Austen ____________________

d) Marie Curie ____________________

e) Adam Smith ____________________

f) Winston Churchill ____________________

g) The Dalai Lama ____________________

h) Stephen Hawking ____________________

i) Pythagoras ____________________

Übung 3: **Die Schule beginnt. Ergänzen Sie:**

Most children in anglophone countries ____________ kindergarten or first grade at age five or six. They ____________ many different kind of classes and ____________ about a lot of different subjects. They ____________ school at around age 18 and then either ____________ an apprenticeship or traineeship or ____________ at the university.

finish
learn
start (x2)
study
take

Apprenticeships:

to do an apprenticeship
to be an apprentice baker | carpenter | machinist

University studies:

to study at the university
to attend a lecture | class |seminar
to take a physics | literature | Japanese class
to do a course in history | to major in history
areas of study | major subjects: law, medicine, computer science ...

!

Note	mark	grade
Schüler/in	pupil	student

Übung 4: Nummerieren Sie die richtige Reihenfolge.

___ a) take and pass exams
___ b) complete | finish one's studies | apprenticeship
___ c) get a degree | become certified
___ d) start a job | career
___ e) attend courses | gain experience

Übung 5: *do*, *get* oder *take*? Ergänzen Sie.

a) ____________ classes
b) ____________ good marks/grades
c) ____________ an exam/text/quiz
d) ____________ an apprenticeship
e) ____________ a degree
f) ____________ an experiment

Kommunikation

Über Schule und Ausbildung sprechen

Übung 6: **Ordnen Sie die richtige Antwort zu.**

a) What did you want to be when you grew up?
b) Did you always get good marks in school?
c) What were your favourite subjects in school?
d) What did you do after you finished school?
e) How were your teachers?
f) When did you finish school?

___ A About five years ago.
___ B I trained to be a hairdresser and opened up my own salon.
___ C I loved maths and history.
___ D I wanted to be a princess.
___ E They weren't all great, but I really liked my high school geography teacher.
___ F I did pretty well, but I struggled in physics.

Übung 7: **Schreiben Sie einen kurzen Text über Ihre Schulzeit. Nutzen Sie die Fragen aus Übung 5 als Anregungen.**

____

____

____

____

Übung 8: **Alice und Jim treffen sich viele Jahre nach der Schulzeit wieder. Ergänzen Sie:**

chemistry | doing | earning | impressed | laboratory | marks | scholarship | traineeship | university

a) Alice: What did you do after you finished school? Did you go to ______________?
b) Jim: No, I did a ______________ in finance at a multinational company. I wanted to start ______________ money as soon as possible! What did you do?
c) Alice: I was lucky enough to get a ______________ and studied ______________.
d) Jim: Well, of course! You always had the top ______________ in science at school! What are you ______________ now?
e) Alice: I work in a ______________ where my team and I do research on cancer.
f) Jim: Wow, I'm ______________!

Im Restaurant

Good evening, we have a reservation under Khan.

Yes, please follow me. Here's your table. Here's the menu.
...
Have you already decided?

Yes, we'd like to start with... and then have the ...
I'd like the fish. Would it be possible to have rice instead of potatoes?

Yes, no problem! | Yes, with a surcharge of 2£.

Would it be possible to get a new glass | fork? This one is a bit dirty. | It fell on the floor.

Yes, of course, sorry about that. How is everything?

Absolutely delicious! My compliments to the chef!

Would you like something for dessert?

Yes, please. What do you have?
No, thank you. We're stuffed! Could we have the bill, please?

Einladung zum Essen

Übung 9: **Was sagt man in folgenden Situationen? Ergänzen Sie:**

delicious | full | treat | seconds

Situation 1: You'd like to go to lunch with your friend and pay for both of you.

Let's go to lunch this Friday. It's my ______________.

Situation 2: Your meal is very tasty.

It's ______________!

Situation 3: You're not hungry for any more food.

No, thanks. I'm ______________.

Situation 4: The food was great and you'd like some more.

Yes, please, I'd love ______________!

Grammatik

Futur: *will, going to* und *present progressive* als Futur

Vergleichen Sie folgende Aussagen aus dem Comic dieser Lektion:
He's going to fly back to the US in one week.
They're looking forward to meeting you.
I'll ask Nadeem and will let you know.
You'll see. We'll have a splendid time together.

Das **will future** kennen Sie schon aus Lektion 3, man benutzt es, um Versprechungen, Angebote, Bedrohungen und kurzfristige Entscheidungen auszudrücken. Das **going to future** verwendet man, wenn man über feste Zukunftspläne spricht:
What are you going to do after you finish school? – I'm going to celebrate!

Hier kann man auch das present progressive nutzen:
What are you doing this weekend? – I'm spending the weekend in the country.

Man nutzt das **going to future** auch für Vorhersagen, wenn man genügend Anhaltspunkte hat, um ziemlich sicher über die Situation zu sprechen:
I'm really nervous about the exam. – You're going to do great!

Übung 10: Will future oder going to future? Ergänzen Sie mit der richtigen Verbform.

1. This summer my mother and I ____________________ fly to Canada.
2. *(aus dem Comic)* Don't worry, my parents ____________________ eat you.
3. What are you doing this weekend? – I don't know, maybe I ____________________ go to the movies if there's anything good playing.
4. Sarah is pregnant. She ____________________ have a baby.
5. – Oh no! We're out of eggs and I wanted to bake a pie! – Don't worry, I ____________________ get some.
6. The sky's getting dark. It ____________________ rain.

Nebensätze im Englischen

Anders als im Deutschen bleiben Haupt- sowie Nebensätze im Englischen in der Regel in der Subjekt-Verb-Objekt-Reihenfolge.

I could see that he was interested in joining us.
Jack is visiting Nashville because he's a huge fan of country music.
We'll go to the museum while they tour the stadium.
Nadeem and Sophie will attend the concert if the show is not sold out.

Die wichtigsten Konjunktionen für englische Nebensätze sind: after (nach, nachdem), although (obwohl), because (weil), before (bevor), if (ob, wenn), since (seit, seitdem), when (als, wenn), where (wo), while (während)

Aussagen im Englischen fangen häufig mit Nebensätzen an:
Before you leave the hotel, please return the key to the front desk.
Although there are many places to stay in London, I recommend the Sapphire!

Übung 11: Ergänzen Sie den Nebensatz mit der richtigen Konjunktion.

1. I'm going to take a nap at the hotel ______________ you go to the museum.
2. ________________ Sandy was a kid, she played on the school basketball team.
3. ________________ you visit Las Vegas, you should really see New York City first.
4. We want to read more about da Vinci __________________ we love art!
5. _______________ you study hard, you'll probably get good marks.
6. _______________ we'd love to come to the party, we unfortunately have to work.

Gerundium oder Infinitiv?

Das Gerundium kennen schon aus Lektion 4 (nach like, love, hate, prefer). Nach manchen Verben im Englischen darf nur das Gerundium stehen. Die wichtigsten dieser Verben sind: avoid (vermeiden), begin (beginnen), consider (sich überlegen), delay (verzögern), discuss (besprechen), dislike (nicht mögen), enjoy (genießen), finish (beenden), involve (beinhalten), keep (mit etwas weitermachen), mention (erwähnen), miss (vermissen), recommend (empfehlen)

Would you recommend going to this restaurant? – No, I would avoid eating there. They received bad reviews.
Have you ever considered studying at the university? – It's not for me. I don't enjoy doing homework.

Übung 12: Gerundium oder Infinitiv? Ergänzen Sie mit der richtigen Verbform.

1. I wish they wouldn't keep _________________ (do) that!
2. My aunt and uncle discussed ________________ (travel) to Australia next year.
3. My brother wanted ________________ (study) sociology, but he got a degree in computer science instead.
4. When did you begin ____________________ (learn) English?
5. Have you finished ____________________ (read) that novel yet?
6. Our mum promised __________________ (take) us to the circus!

Übung 13: **Sophie erzählt von ihrer Kindheit. Setzen Sie die Verben in Klammern ins Präteritum.**

When I ______________ *(to be)* little, I ______________ *(to love)* playing with my cat. (Sometimes a little too much!) I ______________ *(to think)* I wanted to be a veterinarian so that I could be around animals all day long. The only problem was that I couldn't stand seeing blood! Because I've always been talented at writing and languages, my parents ______________ *(to suggest)* I study English at the university. I ______________ *(to study)* very hard and ______________ *(to get)* top honors. Still, my first job as a secretary was a challenge. That boss ______________ *(to demand)* a lot from me! I'm proud of how far I've come since then. I've learned a lot. But when my mother and I look at old photos, we can't help but laugh!

10 It's party time!

Wortschatz	Kommunikation	Grammatik
Familienfeste und Glückwünsche Vorbereitungen für ein Fest	Auf eine Einladung reagieren Gefühle Über Geschenke diskutieren	Genitiv Relativsätze Gerundium (Adjektive und Verben mit Präpositionen)

Back in the USA.
Hey Nadeem, I'm over here!
So, did you have a good time?
You can say that again! Sophie is a wonderful woman. We had so much fun in London.
Joe, I've never felt something like this before. I think I'm in love...
I can see that. She got you good, didn't she?
I haven't told you the best part yet. She's going to visit me in a few weeks. Could you help me organize a surprise party for her?
Are you kidding me? Party's my middle name.

Alright boys, we have a few days left until she arrives. Any ideas for the party? How many people should we invite?
Well, I'm in favor of a barbeque party. Nothing beats home-made burgers.
Sounds good. I think we should keep the guest list small. I don't want to overwhelm Sophie with too many strangers.
I'll bring some soda, snacks, party hats and maybe some beer?
I'll prepare the meat and a salad. We can ask Nadia to bring dessert.
Say mom, could you perhaps bake that wonderful naan bread? I'm sure Sophie would love to try it.
This is going to be really cool.

Is the banner hanging high enough?
Welcome
I need to get forks, knives and plates from the kitchen.
Are these benches enough, or should I get some chairs, too?
Maybe I should clean the grill before we start?
Mom, where do you keep the napkins?
Could you make twenty more balloons, please? Do we even have different colors, too?
Would you put the drinks in the fridge?
Oh boy, her plane's almost here!

Wortschatz

Familienfeste und Glückwünsche

Übung 1: Wie heißen die Ereignisse auf den Bildern? Ordnen Sie zu.

1. 
2. 
3. 
4. 
5. 

___ A birth
___ B birthday
___ C wedding
___ D engagement
___ E first day of school

Übung 2: Welcher Glückwunsch passt zu welcher Situation?

Situations:
a) David is turning 50.
b) We're getting married.
c) The first of January
d) Jennifer is in hospital.
e) Daniel sneezes.

Wishes:
___ A Congratulations to you both!
___ B Happy New Year!
___ C Get well soon!
___ D Bless you!
___ E Happy birthday!

Vorbereitungen für ein Fest

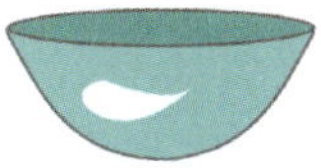
bowl

cup

glass (Plural: glasses)

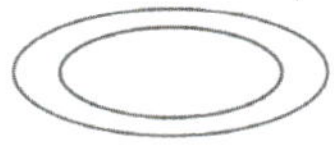
plate

fork

knife (Plural: knives)

spoon

soup plate

Übung 3: Welches Wort fehlt?

a) forks, ____________________, spoons

b) plates, bowls, cups, ________________________

Übung 4: Wie heißen die Tätigkeiten auf den Bildern? Ordnen Sie zu.

1. 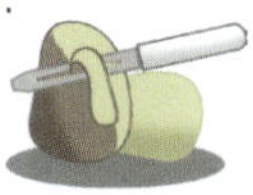

2. 
pan

3. 

4. 

5. 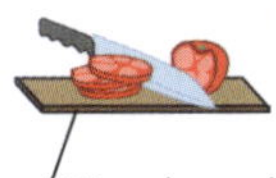
cutting board

6. 
pot

___ A boiling vegetables
___ B baking a cake
___ C frying a sausages
___ D dressing a salad
___ E slicing a tomato
___ F peeling a potato

Andere Verben fürs Kochen

to chop (klein)hacken
to dice würfeln
to grate reiben
to melt schmelzen
to mince hacken

Übung 5: Welches Verb fehlt? Ergänzen Sie:

bake (x2) | boil | fry | grill | make

a) _____________ coffee
b) _____________ a pie
c) _____________ a steak
d) _____________ an omelette
e) _____________ cookies
f) _____________ water

Kommunikation

Auf eine Einladung reagieren

You're invited to a cookout!

LET'S CELEBRATE SUMMER TOGETHER WITH AN OLD-FASHIONED BBQ!

WE'LL BE FIRING UP THE GRILL IN OUR BACKYARD ON SATURDAY, JULY 5TH AT 1 P.M.

WE'LL TAKE CARE OF THE BURGERS, HOT DOGS, AND DRINKS, BUT ANY SIDE DISHES OR DESSERTS YOU COULD BRING WOULD BE MUCH APPRECIATED!

LET US KNOW IF YOU CAN MAKE IT AND WHAT YOU CAN BRING ALONG ☺.

LOOKING FORWARD TO SEEING YOU,
SARAH AND BILL JOHNSON

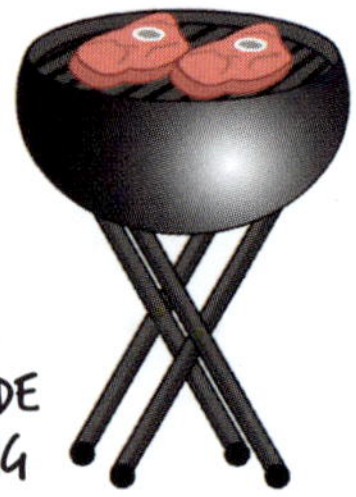

Thank you for the invitation, but unfortunately I'm away that weekend. My sister just had a baby! I hope we'll see each other soon!

Thanks for the invite, I can't wait! I can bring my famous chocolate chip cookies for dessert.

I'd be happy to show up a bit earlier to help you set up.

Sorry, but I'll have to arrive a bit later due to work.

Übung 6: **Und Sie? Sie möchten zur Party kommen. Bedanken Sie sich, sagen Sie, wann Sie kommen, und schreiben Sie auch, was Sie mitbringen.**

Dear

____

____

____

____

____

____

____

See you on Saturday!

Gefühle

1.

angry

2.

scared

3.

sad

4.

in love

5.

disappointed

6.

happy

Übung 7: **Wie fühlt sich Sophie in folgenden Situationen? Ergänzen Sie mit dem richtigen Adjektiv von oben.**

1. Sophie is ____________________ with Nadeem.
2. She's ____________________ when there's bad weather on the weekend.
3. She's ____________________ when she's having fun.
4. She's ____________________ when she watches horror movies.
5. She's ____________________ when people are unkind to her.
6. She's ____________________ when she doesn't get to see Nadeem.

Übung 8: **Beantworten Sie folgende Fragen in ganzen Sätzen auf Englisch.**

1. What makes you angry? ____.
2. Who are you in love with? ____.
3. What is your happiest memory? ____.
4. What movie makes you sad? ____.
5. When are you disappointed? ____.
6. When do you get scared? ____.

Über Geschenke diskutieren

bouquet of flowers

watch

money

jewellery
(US: jewelry)

phone

gift certificate

Danny's turning 10 soon and he wants a smartphone for his birthday. Should we get him one?

No way! He's far too young to have one of those!

I agree, but all of his classmates have one. And it might be useful for emergencies.

Well, that's true. OK, let's get him one.

vorschlagen	positiv reagieren	negativ reagieren
I have an idea... I think we should ... Shall we ... ? Why don't we ... ? What do you think?	That's a great idea! OK. Yes, let's do it! You're | That's right.	No, that's ... That's so boring! No way! No, I think we should ... I have a different idea.

Übung 9: **Ordnen Sie den Dialog.**

___ a) A CD? That's so boring! I have a different idea: why don't we get her a gift certificate for a concert?
___ b) OK, let's do it! You get the gift certificate and I'll get the flowers.
___ c) Why don't we get her some jewellery? What do you think?
___ d) That's a great idea. We should get her a bouquet of flowers, too.
___ e) No, that's too expensive. Let's get her a CD. She loves listening to music.
___ f) What are we getting Laura for her birthday?

Grammatik

Genitiv

Im Vergleich mit dem Deutschen ist der englische Genitiv relativ einfach. Allerdings vergessen viele (auch Muttersprachler!), das Apostroph beim Genitiv zu verwenden.

Bei Substantiven, die kein -s am Ende haben, fügt man ein 's am Ende des Wortes hinzu:	Sophie's parents Nadeem's birthday present Germany's traditions
Bei Substantiven, die ein -s am Ende haben, fügt man entweder nur das Apostroph am Ende oder das 's hinzu - beide Möglichkeiten sind korrekt:	James' party = James's party Christmas' charm = Christmas's charm
Bei Substantiven in der regelmäßigen Mehrzahl fügt man einfach ein Apostroph hinzu:	the girls' toys the Johnsons' barbeque
Bei Substantiven in der unregelmäßigen Mehrzahl fügt man ein 's hinzu:	children's clothes men's shoes

Übung 10: **Bilden Sie den Genitiv des Substantives in Klammern.**

1. ________________ cuisine is famous around the world. (France)
2. ________________ marks were always the best. (Chris)
3. ________________ clothing is upstairs. (women)
4. ________________ parents throw a great party! (Nadeem)
5. My ________________ house is in the countryside. (parents)

Relativpronomen

Relativsätze fangen im Englischen, wie im Deutschen, mit Relativpronomen an. Die wichtigsten davon im Englischen sind: **who** (der, die, das), **whom** (den, die, das), **whose** (dessen, deren), **that** (was, der, die, das), **which** (was, der, die, das), **where** (wo), **when** (wenn).

That nutzt man bei Gegenständen:
I really liked the burgers that we had at the cookout.
Here's the pair of shoes that you wanted.

Who nutzt man bei Menschen:
Is she the friend who lives in South Africa?
Is that the tour guide who(m) we met yesterday?

Whose nutzt man, um Besitz anzuzeigen:
Who is the director whose films we enjoy so much?

Where nutzt man bei Orten:
This is the place where we met.

Übung 11: Ergänzen Sie mit dem richtigen Relativpronomen.

1. There's the cowboy __________ we saw on the street yesterday!
2. Here's the town __________ I grew up.
3. This restaurant, __________ is largest in the area, is celebrating its 100th birthday.
4. Is this a picture of your classmate __________ now lives in Melbourne?
5. That was a time __________ things were simpler.

Das Gerundium nach Adjektiven und Verben mit Präpositionen

Das Gerundium steht nach vielen Adjektiven mit Präpositionen (angry about, good/bad at, disappointed about, happy about, interested in, proud of, tired of) und Verben mit Präpositionen (agree with, believe in, complain about, decide against, look forward to, talk about, think about, worry about):

I was disappointed about not getting a spot at university.
Janet worries about paying the bills.
Tim is good at playing trumpet.
They decided against going out for dinner.

Übung 12: **Beantworten Sie die Fragen in ganzen Sätzen auf Englisch mit einem Gerundium.**

1. What are you looking forward to?

   ____.

2. What are you good at?

   ____.

3. What do you talk about a lot?

   ____.

4. What are you proud of?

   ____.

5. What are you interested in?

   ____.

11

Holiday in the USA

Wortschatz	Kommunikation	Grammatik
Urlaub Ans Meer oder in die Berge? Eine Reise planen	Im Reisebüro Eine Postkarte schreiben	Past progressive Present perfect progressive

So how was your flight? Could you sleep?
No way! I was far too excited!
I give you the Khan residence. After you, Sophie.
Surprise!!
Welcome to America, Sophie!
How did you meet Nadeem?
What do you do for a living?
Welcome
Have you ever been to the US before?
Have you met Nadia yet?

Did you enjoy the party?
Absolutely, everybody was so kind to me... But what did you have in mind for us next?
Have you ever been to the Grand Canyon? I'd love to visit it!
That's a great idea – I went there with my parents when I was a kid; I'd love to see it again.
Alright... I thought about booking a flight to Las Vegas, then renting a car for a road trip to the Grand Canyon...
Sounds great.
and then all the way back to Chicago...
Las Vegas
stopping at any place you want along the way.
Let's do this!

WELCOME
TO Fabulous
LAS VEGAS
NEVADA

Excuse me, could you tell us the way to Bullhead City?

We'd like American breakfast with fried bacon just for her. Eggs sunny side up for us both, please.

BADWATER BASIN
282 FEET / 85.5 METERS
BELOW SEA LEVEL

ROUTE 66 ROCKER
Do you have a double room for tonight?
The time went by far too quickly. I wish you could stay longer.
I know... But you know I have to get back...
Take care, honey... I'll try to visit you as soon as I can...
Bye Nadeem...

Wortschatz

Urlaub

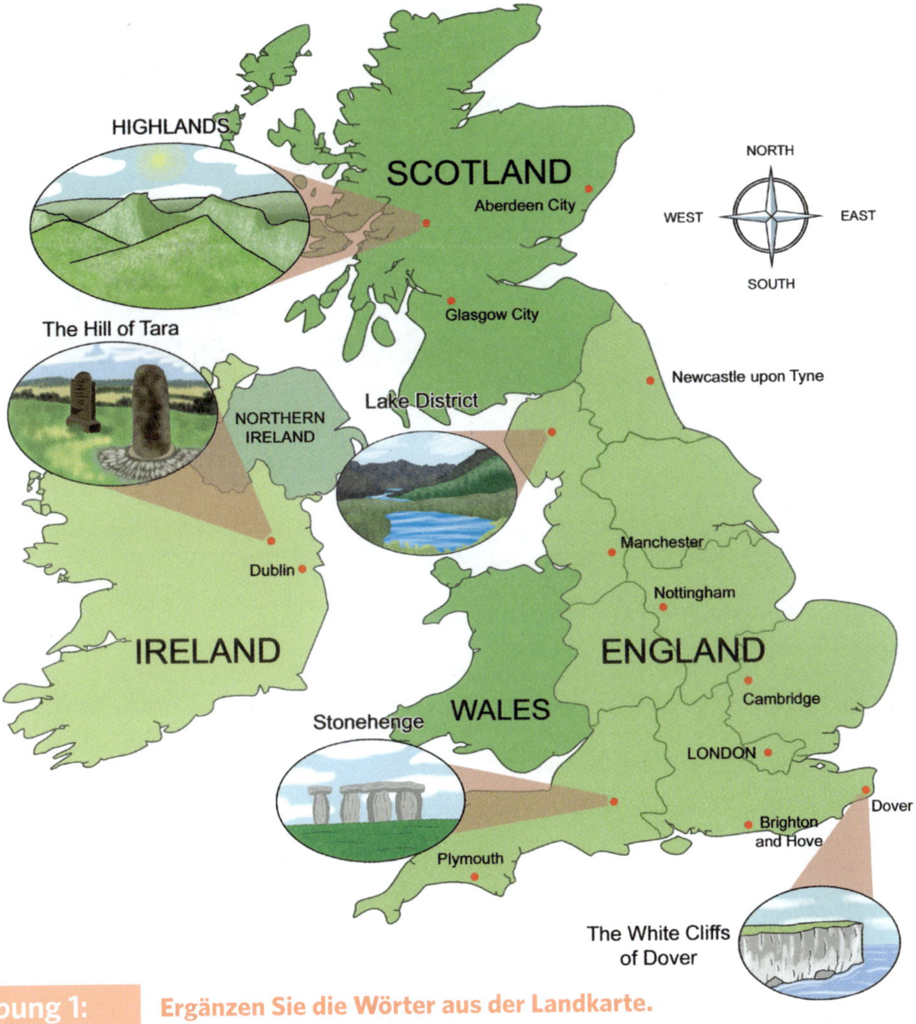

Übung 1: **Ergänzen Sie die Wörter aus der Landkarte.**

The UK and Ireland are wonderful countries to visit on holiday! There's fantastic hiking to be done in the Scottish ______________ in the north and, for archaeology lovers, the ______________ in the east of Ireland. While visiting London, be sure to book a day trip to ______________ west of the capital. Breathtaking views of the English Channel can be seen from the ______________ in England's south. But for visitors who want both water and forest, nothing beats the ______________.

Ans Meer oder in die Berge?

1.

city trip

2.

beach holiday
(US: beach vacation)

3.

hiking trip

4.

cruise

5.

overseas trip

6.

ski trip

Übung 2: Welcher Urlaub passt? Ordnen Sie zu.

a) relaxing at the beach and swimming in the ocean ___
b) skiing or snowboarding in the mountains ___
c) take a ship to visit different ports and islands ___
d) flying to faraway countries ___
e) sightseeing in a city ___
f) hiking in the forest or the mountains ___

> ! take a holiday | a vacation
> a cruise | a trip

Übung 3: Eine Aktivität passt nicht. Kreuzen Sie an.

a) **In the ocean:**
- ☐ swimming
- ☐ climbing
- ☐ diving

b) **In the mountains:**
- ☐ climbing
- ☐ sailing
- ☐ hiking

c) **In the forest:**
- ☐ cycling
- ☐ hiking
- ☐ diving

d) **At the beach:**
- ☐ flying
- ☐ sunbathing
- ☐ swimming

climbing

swimming

hiking

sailing

diving

Eine Reise planen

hotel

bed and breakfast

double room at a hotel

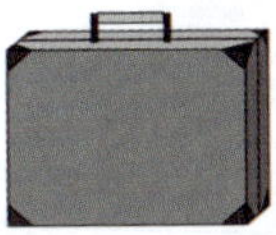
suitcase

rucksack (US: backpack)

travel guide

map

city map

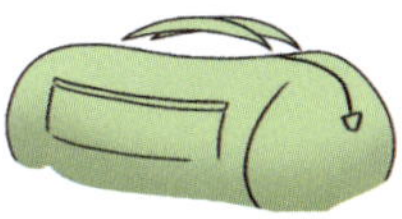
duffel bag

Übung 4: Was muss man planen? Ergänzen Sie:

alone | baggage | bed and breakfast | plane | single

a) What kind of accommodation? A hotel or a small _______________?

b) What type of room? A _______________ room, a double room, or my friend's guest room?

c) What _______________? A suitcase, duffel bag, or a rucksack?

d) Who's coming along? Family members, friends, or travelling _______________?

e) How are we getting there? By car, _______________ or train?

Übung 5: Ordnen Sie die Verben zu. Bei manchen Verben gibt es mehrere Möglichkeiten.

a) a suitcase	___ A to book
b) a travel guide	___ B to buy
c) an accommodation	___ C to pack
d) a holiday | a vacation	___ D to plan
e) a flight	

Kommunikation

Im Reisebüro

I'd like to book a holiday | an inexpensive flight to ...
Could you please tell me about any special offers you have?

How long would you like your vacation to be?
When would you like to leave | to return?

I'd like to travel the week of 10–17 August.

What kind of accommodation were you considering?

A single | double room at a bed and breakfast | hotel | resort

Übung 6: Ergänzen Sie den Dialog.

accommodation | beach | booking | double | forward |offers | tomorrow| tour |train | trip | week

Customer: Good morning! I'd like to travel to Brighton this summer and was wondering if you had any special ________________?

Travel agent: As a matter of fact we do! But first I need some information about your ________________. How long were you looking to stay?

Customer: One ________________.

Travel agent: We have a package ________________ on offer right now for 800£.

Customer: Does the price include ________________ and the flight?

Travel agent: Yes, the bed and breakfast is right on the ________________ and has beautiful seaside views. The price includes your flight as well as the return ________________ ticket from London to Brighton. Would you like a ________________ room?

Customer: No, a single.

Travel agent: In that case there is a surcharge of 100£ for single rooms. Would you be interested in ________________ this holiday today?

Customer: I'd like some time to think this over. I'll call you back ________________.

Travel agent: Quite alright, I look ________________ to your call.

Eine Postkarte schreiben

Dearest Mum and Dad!
Greetings from Las Vegas! Nadeem and I are having a wonderful holiday in the States. We're enjoying driving on Route 66 in a red vintage convertible in such sunny weather! I've tried many new things in the last couple of days, including American pancakes with syrup for breakfast (not my favourite). But I love how big everything is here: the highway, the landscape, even the furniture! I'll see you soon, but I'm going to miss it here.
Love,
Sophie

Übung 7: **Sie machen Urlaub in Brighton Beach. Schreiben Sie eine Postkarte an Ihre Freunde.**

Denken Sie an: Anrede, Informationen zum Urlaub (wo? Unterkunft? Wetter? Aktivitäten? Eindrücke?), Gruß und Unterschrift

Grammatik

Präteritum und Perfekt: Gebrauch

Past progressive

Mit dem *present progressive* haben Sie sich schon in Lektion 2 vertraut gemacht. Wie das *present progressive* wird das *past progressive* mit **be** und Verbstamm + -ing gebildet. Beim past *progressive brauchen* Sie die Vergangenheitsform von **be**: **was/were**. Das *past progressive* bezeichnet eine fortlaufende Handlung in der Vergangenheit:

We were watching television.

Das *past progressive* wird häufig auch verwendet, wenn man Hintergrundinformationen zu einer anderen Handlung aus Vergangenheit geben möchte:

We were watching television when our mum came home.
I was writing a postcard to you when I was on the train to Dover.

Übung 8: **Ergänzen mit dem Verb in Klammern im past progressive.**

1. ______________ you ______________ history when we first met? (study)
2. I ____________ ________________ (read) a book this morning when the birds started singing.
3. Sophie ______________ ____________________ (work) at the front desk when she met Nadeem.
4. Nadeem ____________ ____________________ (travel) on business when he met Sophie.
5. I ____________ ____________________ (think) about you when you called.

Present perfect progressive

Das *present perfect progressive* wird für fortlaufende Handlungen verwendet, die noch nicht beendet sind. Man bildet das *present perfect progressive* mit **has/have** + **been** + Verbstamm + -ing. Das *present perfect progressive* wird häufig, wie das *present perfect*, in Verbindung mit temporalen Adverbien benutzt:

I've been working on this painting for many weeks now.
She's been going to the gym every day this month.

Übung 9: **Ergänzen Sie mit dem Verb in Klammern im *present perfect progressive*.**

1. I ______________________ (write) this book for years.
2. He______________________ (work) there for the last twelve years.
3. My family ________________________________ (come) to this restaurant every Friday night since I was a kid.
4. I ___________________________________ (say) this for a long time now.
5. People __________________________________ (believe) it for a while.

Konditionalsätze im Englischen

Es gibt zwei wichtige Konditionalsatz-Typen im Englischen: der reale Bedingungssatz der Gegenwart (Typ 1) und der irreale Bedingungssatz der Gegenwart (Typ 2). Bei Typ 1 drückt man „wenn-Sätze" aus, die einen direkten, nachvollziehbaren Bezug auf die Gegenwart haben:
If we don't hurry, we'll be late.
If you're good, we'll get ice cream after school.
Bei Typ 1 verwendet man Präsens im if-Satz und will-Futur im Hauptsatz.

Bei Typ 2 handelt es sich um irreale Vorstellungen, die sich auf die Gegenwart beziehen:
If I won a million dollars, I would buy my dream house.
If she worked harder, she would be far more successful.
Bei Typ 2 verwendet man Präteritum (Simple Past) im if-Satz und would + Infinitiv im Hauptsatz.

Übung 10: **Ergänzen Sie die Sätze mit den Verben in den richtigen Formen.**

1. If I ____________________ (have) more money, I ________________________ (go) on holiday more often. (Typus 2)
2. If we ______________________ (buy) three pizzas, we ____________________________ (get) one free. (Typus 1)
3. If I ______________________ (live) in the city, I __________________________ (be) closer to my office. (Typus 2)
4. If he ____________________ (get) a scholarship, he ______________________ (attend) university. (Typus 1)
5. If you ____________________ (pay) this time, I _________________________ (treat) us to lunch next time. (Typus 1)
6. If she ______________________ (understand) the concept, she ______________________ (explain) it to you. (Typus 2)

Übung 11: **Beantworten Sie die Fragen.**

1. If you had millions, what would you do with it?
2. If you could be anyone in the world, who would you be?
3. If you didn't have to work, what would you do?
4. If you could be king or queen for a day, how would you spend it?

12 Romance 2.0

Wortschatz	Kommunikation	Grammatik
Am Computer Im Internet	Über Medien sprechen E-Mails schreiben	Future progressive Typische Grammatikfehler vermeiden

Oh boy... That was a short night. Let's see if Nadeem is still awake.
Almost every morning, Sophie starts up her laptop.
Loading...
Then she loads her Quack application...
Q
...and enters her account information.
Q
LOGIN
Sophie
****
OK
Once she's logged in, she checks if Nadeem is online.
Q
Sophie
online
Friends list
Barbara
Tom
Nadeem
Stephanie
Boss
Vanessa
I know it's far from perfect, but this is the best we've got. Better than nothing...

Good morning, Sophie! How are you doing?
Good evening, Nadeem. I'm fine, thanks. I woke up a little earlier so we could have more time to talk.
Oh, you're so sweet. But I don't have much time tonight. There are some changes coming up in my job which need a lot of my attention. I'll explain everything as soon as I can, OK?
Oh... Alright. Are you in trouble or something like that?
No, not at all, there's nothing to worry about. But I have to get some sleep, honey.
Good night, Nadeem. Best of luck tomorrow!
Hey... I could've slept in...

Later that day...
This is killing me. He has very little time and so much work to do.
I understand that you're frustrated but did you try to talk to him about it and tell him how you feel?
Of course he knows. I miss him like crazy...
Maybe I should distract you a little and take you out to dinner to cheer you up?
I don't feel like going out...
Come on! Don't be such a downer and join me.
Arg... OK, OK. I'll join you! Just stop choking me.
LITTER
That same weekend...
"Let's go out to dinner", she said... "Let me distract you"... Now I'm sitting in this restaurant and she's not even here... Typical... She didn't even text me. Nothing...

She probably fell asleep in front of the TV again...
Excuse me, but would you come with me, please? You have a phone call.
For me? Are you sure?
I believe so. He mentioned you specifically at this table.
Hello, who is this?
Hi Sophie. It's me, Nadeem.
Nadeem? Why are you calling me at this restaurant?
I just wanted to let you know that your friend won't make it tonight. See you later, sweetie.
What on earth is going on here? That just doesn't make any sense...
Who is sitting at my table? Could it be...

Hi, honey. Surprised?
That's one way of putting it. What are you doing here?
I'm so glad your friend can keep a secret. I've been transferred to London. Permanently.
You mean... You're staying here? Really?
Well... Yeah. Is that OK for you?
Oh, Nadeem!!
I think that means "yes".

Wortschatz

Am Computer

1.

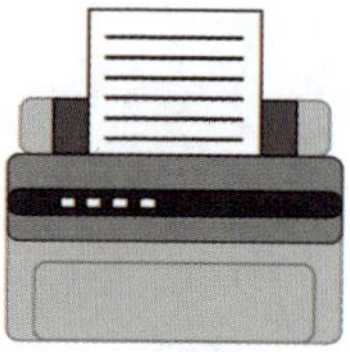

2.

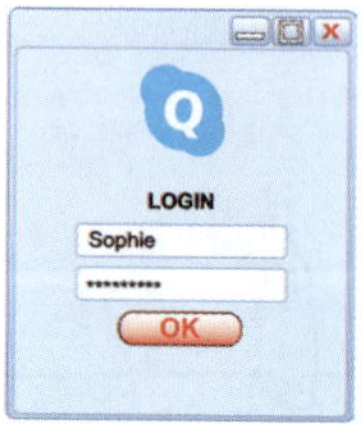

3.

4.

5.

6.

7.

8.

Übung 1: Was ist das? Ergänzen Sie die Nummer.

a) screen ___

b) printer ___

c) account ___

d) laptop ___

e) UK outlet and plug ___

f) US outlet and plug ___

g) keyboard ___

h) mouse ___

Übung 2: Was macht Nadeem, wenn er via Internet mit Sophie sprechen möchte? Nummerieren Sie die richtige Reihenfolge.

___ a) starts his computer

___ b) closes the Quack program

___ c) shuts down his computer

___ d) signs in with his username and password

___ e) opens the Quack program

___ f) chats with Sophie

Im Internet

Übung 3: Was bedeutet das? Schreiben Sie die Wörter unter die Symbole.

close a window | copy | e-mail | file | like | link | open a file | print | save | search

a) ____________

b) ____________

www.pons.de

c) ____________

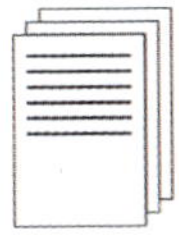

d) ____________

e) ____________

f) ____________

g) ____________

h) ____________

i) ____________

j) ____________

Übung 4: Ein Wort passt nicht in die Reihe. Kreuzen Sie an.

a) ... a file	☐ save	☐ start	☐ open	☐ copy
b) on the internet:	☐ chat	☐ surf	☐ shop	☐ enter
c) ... a message	☐ read	☐ receive	☐ send	☐ shut down
d) ... a photo	☐ surf	☐ print out	☐ post	☐ e-mail

Kommunikation

Über Medien sprechen

radio

the Internet

television (TV)

e-book

smartphone

newspaper

magazine

Übung 5: **Ergänzen Sie das Medium, von dem die Personen sprechen.**

a) After dinner, my family and I like to watch a show on ______________________.

b) At breakfast, Mrs Robinson likes to read the morning ______________________.

c) Many people prefer reading an ____________________ on the tablet instead of reading a paperback.

d) When I cook, I like to listen to music and news programmes on the ___________________.

e) I always want to stay up-to-date, so I only turn off my ____________________ when I go to sleep.

f) Without ________________________, I wouldn't be able to skype with my friends.

g) I only read ______________________ at the doctor's and dentist's office.

E-Mails schreiben

	informell	formell
Anrede	Dear Peter, Dearest Susanne, Hi, | Hey,	Dear President Williams Dear Dr Field *(nicht Mr Dr!)* Dear Mr Robinson Dear Mrs Robinson Dear Ms Smith *(neutraler Ausdruck bei Frauen)*
Im Text	*Contractions erlaubt:* I've we're can't	*Keine contractions:* I have we are can not
Gruß	Best | Warm wishes, All the best, Yours, Love,	Sincerely, Best regards,
Unterschrift	*Nur Vorname*	*Vorname und Nachname*

Übung 6: **Nadeem schreibt folgende Mail an den Präsidenten seiner Firma. Ergänzen Sie:**

director | has | hearing | office | pleasure | President | Sincerely| transfer | trip | would

Subject Line: Request for Transfer to London

Dear ________________ Simons,

My name is Nadeem Khan and I am ________________ of sales for your Chicago branch. It ______________ been my great ____________________ to work for Great Lakes Industries over the past decade and to watch our branch grow successfully under my direction. On a recent business _______________ to London, I visited our operations in the UK and was impressed by what I saw. I _________________ like to be part of that team and would like to hereby request my ______________ to the London ________________.

My resume and application are attached. Thank you very kindly for your consideration. I look forward to __________________ from you.

________________________,
Nadeem Khan

Übung 7:

Beim Schreiben ist es eine gute Idee, sich entweder für das britische oder das amerikanische Englisch zu entscheiden, um Sprachpannen und Missverständnisse zu vermeiden. Nadeem nutzt folgende Wörter, aber wie würde sich Sophie ausdrücken? Übersetzen Sie das US-amerikanische Englisch ins britische Englisch!

1. cookie → ____________
2. eggplant → ____________
3. zucchini → ____________
4. pants → ____________
5. potato chips → ____________
6. soccer → ____________
7. first floor → ____________
8. go on vacation → go on ____________
9. sweater → ____________
10. highway → ____________
11. gas → ____________
12. to stand in line *(Schlange stehen)* → ____________
13. candy → ____________
14. student *(Schüler)* → ____________
15. subway → ____________

Übung 8:

Und wie würde Sophie folgende Wörter buchstabieren?

1. theater → ____________
2. color → ____________
3. organize → ____________
4. jewelry → ____________
5. center → ____________
6. humor → ____________

Übung 9: Falsche Freunde! Was ist die englische Übersetzung folgender Wörter?

1. Noten → ____________________
2. Stadtplan → _________________
3. Handy → ____________________
4. Oldtimer → __________________

Grammatik

Future progressive

In Lektion 11 wurden *past progressive* und *present perfect progressive* besprochen, nun kommen wir zum *future progressive*. Das *future progressive* bildet man mit **will** + **be** + Verbstamm + -ing und verwendet es, wenn man genau schildern möchte, was in Zukunft geschehen wird:

I'll be waiting for you when you arrive at the airport.
We'll be thinking of you every day you are away.

Das *future progressive* ist in manchen Fällen auch einfach eine Alternative zum *going to future* oder *present progressive* als Futur:

We'll be going away this weekend. = We're going away this weekend.
Tomorrow I'll be giving my presentation to the group. = Tomorrow I'm giving my presentation to the group.

Übung 10: **Ergänzen Sie das Verb in Klammern im future progressive.**

1. I ______________________________ (writing) e-mails while you are on the phone.
2. Our daughter ______________________________ (start) her first semester of university this fall.
3. You ______________________________ (study) while I'm asleep
4. The professor ______________________________ (offer) three courses this semester.
5. This author ______________________________ (sign) her books after the reading.

Übung 11: **Beantworten Sie die Frage in einem ganzen Satz auf Englisch.**

What will you be doing with your English after finishing this course?

____

____.

Häufige Fehler von deutschsprachigen Englischlernern - und wie man sie vermeidet

1. Bestimmter Artikel oder Null-Artikel? Zählbar oder unzählbar?

Viele deutsche Substantive, die Abstraktionen bezeichnen (wie z.B. *die Gesellschaft, die Natur, die amerikanische Kultur*), nutzen den bestimmten Artikel, aber er ist in diesen Fällen im Englischen fehl am Platz (**society**, **nature**, **American culture**). Es gibt auch zählbare Substantive im Deutschen (wie *Hausaufgaben, Informationen, Ratschläge*), die wiederum unzählbar im Englischen sind (**homework**, **information**, **advice**).

Übung 12: **Übersetzen Sie ins Englische!**

1. Meine Schwester gibt mir immer die besten Ratschläge.

___________________________________.

2. Ich liebe die Natur!

___________________________________!

3. Vielen Dank für die Informationen!

___________________________________!

4. Wir sind von der britischen Kultur fasziniert.

___________________________________.

5. Ohne die Kunst ist das Leben nur halb so schön.

___________________________________.

2. present perfect (Perfekt) vs. simple past (Präteritum)

Da man auf Deutsch Vergangenes im Gespräch mit dem Perfekt ausdrückt, neigt man dazu, das auch auf Englisch zu machen. Dabei funktioniert das Perfekt im Englischen deutlich anders: Es darf nur in Fällen verwendet werden, die noch aktuell sind. Adverbien wie **ever** oder **still** weisen auf das Perfekt hin. Handlungen, die abgeschlossen sind, müssen mit dem Präteritum ausgedrückt werden.

Übung 13: **Übersetzen Sie ins Englische.**

1. Letzten Sommer habe ich in der Schweiz verbracht.

___________________________________.

2. Als ich ein Kind war, spielte ich Geige.

___________________________________.

3. Haben Sie diesen Film schon mal gesehen?

___________________________________?

4. Wir kennen uns seit längerer Zeit.

___________________________________.

5. Was hast du am Wochenende gemacht?

___________________________________?

3. simple vs. progressive

Da das Deutsche das *progressive* nicht kennt, neigt der Deutschsprachige dazu, zu häufig das Präsens zu verwenden oder das *progressive* falsch anzuwenden. Handlungen im *progressive* sind Prozesse und keine Zustände. Da das *present progressive* auch Zukunftspläne ausdrücken kann, wird es häufiger benutzt als man denkt.

Übung 14: **Simple oder progressive? Schreiben Sie das Verb in Klammern in der richtigen Form.**

1. Yes, that (make) sense!

   ______________________________!

2. I (go) to the store now.

   ______________________________.

3. We (know) each other.

   ______________________________.

4. I (think) about you.

   ______________________________!

5. She (feel) bad about it.

   ______________________________.

4. Genitiv-s und Großschreibung

Da im Englischen im Vergleich zum Deutschen ja sehr vieles klein geschrieben wird, neigt man dazu, auch da klein zu schreiben, wo eigentlich Großschreibung richtig wäre, z.B. beim Pronomen „I", bei Länder- oder Sprachenbezeichnungen. Auch das Apostroph beim englischen Genitiv ist unabdingbar.

Übung 15: **Schreiben Sie die Sätze mit korrekter Zeichensetzung und Groß-/Kleinschreibung.**

1. M Y F A M I L Y L O V E S G E R M A N F O O D

   ____

2. W E W E R E P L E A S E D W I T H T H E C L A S S E S G R A D E S

   ____

3. I M S T U D Y I N G M A T H S E N G L I S H A N D P H Y S I C S

   ____

4. J E S S P A R T I E S A R E A L W A Y S T H E H I G H L I G H T O F T H E Y E A R

   ____

5. M Y F A V O U R I T E H O L I D A Y I S C H R I S T M A S

   ____

5. Reflexive Verben

Das Englische hat deutlich weniger reflexive Verben als das Deutsche. Verben wie *sich rasieren* oder *sich etwas vorstellen* werden mit „to shave“ und „to imagine“ ins Englische übersetzt. Hier ein paar andere Beispiele:

sich schminken	to do one's makeup
sich die Zähne putzen	to brush one's teeth
sich ärgern	to get angry
sich ändern	to change

Übung 16: **Übersetzen Sie ins Englische!**

1. Ich wasche mir die Hände. ____.
2. Wir interessieren uns für Städtereisen. ____.
3. Treffen wir uns morgen? ____?
4. Mach du dir keine Sorgen! ____!

Congratulations on finishing the course!

Unregelmäßige Verben

Verb	Partizip
be	been
become	become
begin	begun
break	broken
bring	brought
build	built
catch	caught
choose	chosen
came	come
cost	cost
cut	cut
do	done
drink	drunk
drive	driven
eat	eaten
fall	fallen
feed	fed
feel	felt
fight	fought
find	found
fly	flown
forget	forgotten
get	got (BrE) / gotten (AmE)
give	given
go	gone
grow	grown
have	had
hear	heard
hold	held
keep	kept
know	known
lead	led
leave	left
lend	lent
let	let
lose	lost
make	made
mean	meant

meet	met
pay	paid
put	put
read	read [rɛd]
ride	ridden
ring	rung
run	run
say	said [sɛd]
see	seen
sell	sold
send	sent
set	set
steal	stolen
show	shown
sing	sung
sit	set
sleep	slept
speak	spoken
spend	spent
stand	stood
swim	swum
take	taken
teach	taught
tell	told
think	thought
understand	understood
wear	worn
win	won
write	written

Lösungen

Lektion 1

Übung 1
a) Poland • b) Norwegian • c) Russian • d) Germany, Austria, Switzerland • e) Turkish • f) French • g) Japan • h) Spanish

Übung 2

A	F	O	U	R	N	A	E	U	W	G	O	P	X	S
U	D	N	O	F	I	F	T	E	E	N	I	H	P	E
B	F	E	F	N	I	O	W	K	S	A	V	J	R	V
S	C	W	B	I	Y	S	E	V	T	W	E	L	V	E
I	D	F	G	U	Q	I	N	O	Q	H	J	F	K	N
X	T	Z	A	D	V	X	T	L	S	A	D	E	L	T
T	R	N	F	I	F	T	Y	-	F	I	V	E	L	Y
Y	U	X	C	G	B	E	A	C	V	H	U	I	K	-
-	E	J	K	F	H	E	W	T	U	R	C	G	L	T
O	A	H	K	L	L	N	E	Z	I	O	G	H	K	W
N	V	C	E	U	M	C	G	D	G	H	N	T	E	O
E	D	F	J	K	I	E	L	E	V	E	N	Y	A	B

Übung 3
1 twenty-seven • 2 forty • 3 eighteen • 4 fifty-seven • 5 thirty-three • 6 seventeen

Übung 4
b, d, e, c, a

Übung 5
is, director, works, it's, pleasure, happy

Übung 6
1 Who are you? • 2 What is it? • 3 Where are they? • 4 How are you?

Übung 7
1 D • 2 A • 3 G • 4 F • 5 H • 6 C • 7 E • 8 B

Übung 8
individuelle Antworten

Übung 9
a) you • b) you • c) He • d) she • e) you, I

Übung 10
a) a • b) the • c) the, the • d) an • e) a

Übung 11
a) come • b) Are • c) teaches • d) speaks • e) live • f) are • g) goes

Übung 12
b) lives • c) comes from • d) is • e) works • f) speaks

Übung 13
individuelle Antworten

Übung 14
b) What is your native language? • c) My surname is Williamson. • d) Does she speak German? • e) Do you live in Glasgow? • f) I speak a little English.

Lektion 2

Übung 1
a) sky, blue • b) white, sun • c) grass, trees • d) yellow

Übung 2
a) blue, red, white • b) green, white, orange • c) blue, white • d) red, green, white • e) black, red, yellow (gold)

Übung 3
a) autumn/fall • b) spring • c) winter • d) summer

Übung 4
1 e • 2 a • 3 b • 4 d • 5 c

Übung 5
Individuelle Antworten

Übung 6
c, g, d, a, e, b, f

Übung 7
mögliche Antwort: In my free time, I paint and play the guitar. I also like going cycling.

Übung 8
a) cities • b) stars • c) birds • d) wishes • e) sandwiches • f) lives • g) gases • h) taxes

Übung 9
a) are you going • b) is Sophie doing • c) is going • d) is playing • e) am not reading

Übung 10
a) like • b) am reading • c) has • d) am having

Übung 11
1 c • 2 b • 3 d • 4 a

Übung 12
a) Our • b) His • c) your, my • d) her • e) Their

Lektion 3

Übung 1
a) Monday, Friday • b) Saturday, Sunday

Übung 2
a) seven hundred eighty • b) one thousand fifty-six • c) seventeen hundred/ one thousand seven hundred • d) eighteen "o" eight • e) eighteen thirty-seven • f) two thousand eleven

Übung 3
b) Today is the fifth of April. Today is April fifth. • c) Today is the eleventh of November. Today is November eleventh. • e) I am leaving for Dublin on the second of July. I am leaving for Dublin on July second. • f) I am leaving for Dublin on the eighteenth of June. I am leaving for Dublin on June eighteenth. • h) I was born on thirty-first of January nineteen ninety-six. I was born on January thirty-first nineteen ninety-six. • i) I was born on the second of October two thousand two. I was born on October second two thousand two.

Übung 4
a) 5 • b) 3 • c) 6 • d) 4 • e) 2

Übung 5
e, d, f, b, c, a

Übung 6
a) ten to six • b) a quarter past eight

Übung 7
do, have, will, sounds, I'll, looking

Übung 8
a) B • b) C • c) A • d) D

Übung 9
1 her • 2 them • 3 me • 4 it • 5 us

Übung 10
a) In • b) on, at • c) from, to • d) in

Übung 11
mögliche Antworten:
a) Yes, I have two sons. • b) No, I'm going to the cinema on Sunday. • c) No, I have three cats. • d) Yes, I'm working today until 5 p.m. • e) No, I'm cooking at home. • f) No, I prefer tea. • g) No, I go to the gym three days a week.

Übung 12
a) He can play the guitar. • b) How many languages can she speak? • c) When should we be at the train station? • d) Could you please close/shut the window? • e) Mummy, may I play with my friends?

Übung 13
a) can't • b) should not • c) could • d) could

Übung 14
a) would like • b) want • c) would like • d) want, wants

Lektion 4

Übung 1
body, tall, muscular, short, blond, eyes, funny

Übung 2
1) Abraham Lincoln • 2) Marilyn Monroe • 3) Bruce Willis • 4) Frank Sinatra • 5) Steve Jobs

Übung 3
individuelle Antworten

Übung 4
1 long • 2 muscular • 3 serious • 4 tall, slim, skinny • 5 teeth • 6 dull, funny

Übung 5
a) shorts, T-shirt • b) boots, coat, mittens, hat, scarf • c) blouse, skirt, trousers • d) suit, shirt, tie

Übung 6
a) short • b) loose • c) dark • d) cheap • e) old • f) dull • g) short • h) plain • i) skinny • j) old-fashioned • k) uncomfortable • l) ugly

Übung 7
a) loose • b) tight • c) expensive • d) big

Übung 8
e, d, i, b, f, h, c, g, a

Übung 9
individuelle Antworten

Übung 10
individuelle Antworten

Übung 11
1 too sweet • 2 too tight • 3 very nice • 4 quite short

Lektion 5

Übung 1
a) 4 • b) 8 • c) 3 • d) 5 • e) 2 • f) 1 • g) 7 • h) 6

Übung 2
1 roll • 2 bread • 3 butter • 4 egg • 5 honey • 6 cheese • 7 jam • 8 milk • 9 coffee • 10 tea • 11 sausage • 12 sugar

Übung 3
mögliche Antworten: a) I need thirty minutes. • b) It takes me twenty minutes by car. • c) I work until 3 p.m. on Fridays. • d) I usually sleep in until 10 a.m. at the weekend.

Übung 4
individuelle Antworten

Übung 5
waiter: b, c, d, e, f, i guest: a, g, h, j, k

Übung 6
a) D • b) A • c) E • d) B • e) C

Übung 7
individuelle Antworten

Übung 8
a) morning, o'clock • b) take • c) make breakfast, newspaper • d) take, hour • e) office • f) lunch • g) afternoon • h) home • i) groceries • j) dinner • k) watch • l) bed

Übung 9
individuelle Antworten

Übung 10
a) funniest • b) more • c) warmer, warmest • d) better • e) faster • f) longer • g) nicest

Übung 11
a) as • b) than • c) as • d) than • e) than

Übung 12
1) She never eats meat. • 2) He rarely watches TV. • 3) They are always on time. • 4) I rarely go dancing. • 5) He frequently goes to the movies./He goes to the movies frequently. • 6) She writes poetry sometimes./ Sometimes she writes poetry./She sometimes writes poetry.

Übung 13
1) I'm getting really angry now! • 2) It gets darker and colder in the winter. • 3) I need to get milk and bread at the supermarket. • 4) My little brother gets taller (with) every year. • 5) How do you get there?

Übung 14
1) a • 2) a • 3) c

Übung 15
1) take/make • 2) have/take • 3) have

Lektion 6

Übung 1
a) motorway • b) pedestrian zone • c) parking space • d) traffic light • e) zebra crossing • f) bridge

Übung 2
a) 3 • b) 1, 3 • c) 2 • d) 4 • e) 1

Übung 3
train station

Übung 4
a) Take Greenford Rd and go straight until you see the traffic light, then turn left on Stratford Rd. The cinema is on the left-hand side of the street.
b) Take Station Rd and turn left on Brick Lane. Go straight until you see the traffic light, then turn right on Johnston St. Go straight and you'll see Greenford Rd. (You can't miss it, the station is right there.)

Übung 5
a) F • b) D • c) C • d) E • e) B • f) A • g) G

Übung 6
1) Nadeem asked a man for directions. • 2) Nadeem took the tube. • 3) He rode the bus. • 4) He spoke with an elderly woman. • 5) He arrived at the café. • 6) He visited the London Eye. • 7) He enjoyed the view from the top.

Übung 7
1) She walked to school. • 2) He called his friends on the phone. • 3) We wanted to go on holiday. • 4) They live in Leicester. • 5) I preferred cake over chips. • 6) You worried about me.

Übung 8
1) forgot • 2) saw • 3) got • 4) wrote • 5) taught • 6) ate • 7) was • 8) were • 9) went • 10) could, was

Übung 9
Mögliche Antwort:
Last year on holiday I went to Washington D.C. with my family. We had a great time. We visited lots of museum and saw the White House. We ate traditional American food and listened to rock music at a concert.

Übung 10
1) We didn't go to school on foot. • 2) They didn't sing traditional songs. • 3) The meal didn't cost a lot. • 4) The group didn't choose a fascinating book. • 5) I didn't think so. • 6) She didn't send the package on time.

Lektion 7

Übung 1
Mögliche Antworten:
a) I live on the first floor. • b) My house has five rooms. • c) Yes, my apartment has a balcony. • d) I have a garden, but I don't have a basement or a cellar.

Übung 2
a) living room • b) bathroom • c) kitchen • d) bedroom • e) dining room

Übung 3
b) blanket • c) shelf • d) curtain • e) stove • f) dishes • g) rug • h) mirror

Übung 4
A) d • B) g • C) h • D) c • E) f • F) a • G) b • H) e

Übung 5
Mögliche Antwort:
My dream house is in the countryside and has a huge garden with lots of flowers. The house has two floors with a big kitchen with a beautiful view. The house has three bedrooms with large closets, two bathrooms (one with a big bathtub), a living room with tall windows, an attic, and a basement.

Übung 6
a) 5 • b) 7 • c) 2 • d) 9 • e) 8 • f) 4 • g) 1 • h) 6 • i) 3

Übung 7
A) i • B) a • C) c • D) h • E) b • F) d • G) e • H) f • I) j • J) g

Übung 8
a) on, next to • b) in, between • c) next to • d) under • e) in front of • f) behind

Übung 9
1) washed • 2) completed • 3) talked • 4) moved • 5) lived

Übung 10
1) won • 2) fed • 3) sung • 4) written • 5) eaten • 6) seen • 7) slept • 8) spoken • 9) known • 10) begun

Übung 11
1. I've never eaten anything more delicious! • 2) We went to the cinema at the weekend/this past weekend. • 3) We've already gone to this restaurant many times. • 4) I saw her recently. • 5) Last summer we went to Crete on holiday.

Übung 12

are not	aren't	we are	we're
can not	can't	they are	they're
could not	couldn't	she has	she's
do not	don't	I have	I've
should not	shouldn't	we have	we've
were not	weren't	they have	they've
will not	won't	he will	he'll
it is	it's	I will	I'll
he is	he's	we will	we'll
I am	I'm	they will	they'll

Lektion 8

Übung 1
a) potatoes • b) noodles • c) lettuce • d) fish • e) rice

Übung 2
bakery, butcher's, market, supermarket, drink shop

Übung 3
a) jar • b) can • c) package • d) bottle • e) bottle • f) box • g) bag

Übung 4
Mögliche Antwort: In the summer, I like to make fruit salad. To make it, you need one pound of strawberries, one pound of cherries, and a little bit of lemon juice. Sometimes I add apples.

Übung 5
a) ear • b) nose • c) mouth • d) neck • e) eye

Übung 6
a) hands • b) stomach • c) back • d) feet • e) chest • f) head • g) knees

Übung 7
7, 2, 5, 4, 1, 3, 6

Übung 8
a) 2 • b) 3 • c) 1 • d) 3 • e) 1 • f) 2

Übung 9
a) 1 • b) 2, 3 • c) 1 • d) 1, 2, 3

Übung 10
a) 6 • b) 3 • c) 1 • d) 8 • e) 5 • f) 4 • g) 2 • h) 7

Übung 11
a) 1 • b) 6 • c) 4 • d) 2 • e) 5 • f) 7 • g) 3

Übung 12
Cook, Fry, Stir, Simmer, Mix, Layer, Bake

Übung 13
a) Drink more tea! • b) Eat more fruit! • c) Be there at 2 p.m.! • d) Don't be late!

Übung 14
a) much • b) many • c) few • d) little • e) few

Lektion 9

Übung 1
a) journalist • b) hair dresser, hair stylist • c) carpenter • d) teacher • e) veterinarian • f) salesperson • g) scientist • h) mechanic • i) bank clerk

Übung 2
a) art • b) geography • c) English • d) chemistry • e) economics • f) history • g) religion • h) physics • i) math(s)

Übung 3
start, take, learn, finish, start, study

Übung 4
a) 4 • b) 3 • c) 4 • d) 5 • e) 1

Übung 5
a) Take • b) get • c) do/take • d) do • e) get/do • f) do

Übung 6
A) f • B) d • C) c • D) a • E) e • F) b

Übung 7
individuelle Antworten

Übung 8
university, traineeship, earning, scholarship, chemistry, marks, doing, laboratory, impressed

Übung 9
treat, delicious, full, seconds

Übung 10
1) am going to • 2) won't • 3) will • 4) is going to • 5) will • 6) is going to

Übung 11
1) while • 2) When • 3) Before • 4) because • 5) If • 6) Although

Übung 12
1) doing • 2) travelling • 3) to study • 4) learning • 5) reading • 6) to take

Übung 13
was, loved, thought, suggested, studied, got, demanded

Lektion 10

Übung 1
A) 3 • B) 5 • C) 2 • D) 4 • E) 1

Übung 2
A) b • B) c • C) d • D) e • E) a

Übung 3
a) knives • b) glasses

Übung 4
A) 6 • B) 3 • C) 2 • D) 4 • E) 5 • F) 1

Übung 5
a) make • b) bake • c) grill • d) fry • e) bake • f) boil

Übung 6
individuelle Antworten

Übung 7
1) in love • 2) disappointed • 3) happy • 4) scared • 5) angry • 6) sad

Übung 8
mögliche Antworten:
1) Unkind people make me angry. • 2) I'm in love with life! • 3) My happiest memory is having my son/daughter. • 4) Casablanca makes me sad. • 5) I'm most disappointed when the train is not on time. • 6) I get scared when I'm alone at night in a city I don't know.

Übung 9
a) 4 • b) 6 • c) 2 • d) 5 • e) 3 • f) 1

Übung 10
1) France's • 2) Chris'/Chris's • 3) Women's • 4) Nadeem's • 5) parents'

Übung 11
1) who(m) • 2) where • 3) which • 4) who • 5) when

Übung 12
mögliche Antworten:
1) I'm looking forward to going on holiday this summer. • 2) I'm good at playing the piano. • 3) I talk a lot about going to Australia one day. • 4) I'm proud of reading so much. • 5) I'm interested in taking more language classes.

Lektion 11

Übung 1
Highlands, Hill of Tara, Stonehenge, White Cliffs of Dover, Lake District

Übung 2
a) 2 • b) 6 • c) 4 • d) 5 • e) 1 • f) 3

Übung 3
a) In the ocean: swimming, diving • b) In the mountains: climbing, hiking • c) In the forest: cycling, hiking • d) At the beach: sunbathing, swimming

Übung 4
a) bed and breakfast • b) single • c) baggage • d) alone • e) plane

Übung 5
A) c, d, e • B) a, b • C) a, b • D) d, e

Übung 6
offers, trip, week, tour, accommodation, beach, train, double, booking, tomorrow, forward

Übung 7
individuelle Antworten

Übung 8
1) Were you studying • 2) I was reading • 3) Sophie was working • 4) Nadeem was travelling • 5) I was thinking

Übung 9
1) I have been writing • 2) He has been working • 3) My family has been coming • 4) I have been saying

Übung 10
1) had, would go • 2) buy, will get • 3) lived, would be • 4) gets, will attend • 5) pay, will treat • 6) understood, would explain

Übung 11
mögliche Antworten: 1) If I had millions, I would travel the world! • 2) If I could be anyone in the world, I would still be me! • 3) If I didn't have to work, I would spend more time reading. • 4) If I could be king or queen for the day, I would give everyone the day off!

Lektion 12

Übung 1
a) 3 • b) 1 • c) 2 • d) 7 • e) 4 • f) 5 • g) 6 • h) 8

Übung 2
a) 1 • b) 5 • c) 6 • d) 3 • e) 2 • f) 4

Übung 3
a) search • b) print • c) link • d) copy • e) e-mail • f) open a file • g) close a window • h) like • i) save • j) file

Übung 4
a) start • b) enter • c) shut down • d) surf

Übung 5
a) television • b) newspaper • c) e-book • d) radio • e) smartphone • f) the Internet • g) magazines

Übung 6
President, director, has, pleasure, trip, would, transfer, office, hearing, Sincerely

Übung 7
1) biscuit • 2) aubergine • 3) courgette • 4) trousers • 5) crisps • 6) football • 7) ground floor • 8) holiday • 9) jumper • 10) motorway • 11) petrol • 12) to queue • 13) sweets • 14) pupil • 15) Tube

Übung 8
1) theatre • 2) colour • 3) organise • 4) jewellery • 5) centre • 6) humour

Übung 9
1) marks, grades • 2) city map • 3) mobile phone • 4) vintage car

Übung 10
1) will be writing • 2) will be starting • 3) will be studying • 4) will be offering • 5) will be signing

Übung 11
individuelle Antworten

Übung 12
1) My sister always gives the best advice. • 2) I love nature! • 3) Thank you very much for the information. • 4) We are fascinated by British culture. • 5) Life is only half as lovely without art./Without art, life is only half as lovely.

Übung 13
1) We spent last summer in Switzerland. • 2) When I was a child, I played violin. • 3) Have you ever seen this film? • 4) We've known each other for a while. • 5) What did you do at the weekend?

Übung 14
1) Yes, that makes sense! • 2) I'm going to the store now. • 3) We know each other. • 4) I'm thinking about you. • 5) She feels bad about it.

Übung 15
1) My family loves German food. • 2) We were pleased with the classes' grades. • 3) I'm studying maths, English, and physics. • 4) Jess' parties are always the highlight of the year. • 5) My favourite holiday is Christmas.

Übung 16
1) I'm washing my hands. / I wash my hands. • 2) We're interested in city trips. • 3) Shall we meet (up) tomorrow? • 4) Don't worry!

Alphabetische Wortliste

In der Wortliste finden Sie alle Wörter aus dem Comic und aus den Übungen. Zahlen, Grammatikbegriffe und Namen (zum Beispiel von Personen, Städten, Seen, ...) stehen nicht in der Liste.
Ein / nach einem Präfix bedeutet: Das Verb ist trennbar.
(Sg.) bedeutet: Das Wort gibt es nur im Singular; (Pl.): Das Wort gibt es nur im Plural.
Andere Abkürzungen: Akk. = Akkusativ, Dat. = Dativ, Gen. = Genitiv.

A

a	*ein, eine, eins*
a.m.	*Vormittag*
abbey	*Kloster, Abtei*
about	*über; wegen; ungefähr*
above	*über, oberhalb*
absolutely	*absolut*
accent	*Akzent*
accommodation	*Unterkunft*
account	*Konto*
to acquire	*erwerben*
actually	*tatsächlich, eigentlich*
address	*Adresse*
adult	*Erwachsene/r*
adventure	*Abenteuer*
adventurous	*abenteuerlich*
advert, advertisement	*Werbeanzeige, Werbespot*
advice	*Ratschlag*
aeroplane (BE)	*Flugzeug*
to afford	*sich leisten*
affordable	*bezahlbar*
afraid	*verängstigt, ängstlich*
after	*nach(dem)*
afternoon	*Nachmittag*
afterwards	*danach, nachher, später*
again	*wieder*
against	*gegen*
age	*Alter*
ago	*vor, früher*
to agree	*zustimmen, sich einig werden*
air	*Luft*
airline	*Fluggesellschaft*
airplane (AE)	*Flugzeug*
aisle	*Gang*
alcohol	*Alkohol*
all	*alle(s)*
all day	*den ganzen Tag*
all the way	*den ganzen Weg*
almost	*fast*
alone	*allein*
along	*entlang*
already	*schon*
alright	*in Ordnung, OK, gut*
also	*auch*
although	*obwohl*
always	*immer*
America	*Amerika*
American	*amerikanisch, Amerikaner/in*
amputation	*Amputation*
and	*und*
angry	*böse, ärgerlich*
animal	*Tier*
ankle	*Knöchel*
annoyed	*genervt, verärgert*
another	*ein andere/r/s*
answer	*Antwort*
to answer	*antworten*
anything	*irgendetwas*
Anything else?	*Sonst noch etwas? Sonst noch ein Wunsch?*
apart from	*abgesehen von, außer*
apartment	*Wohnung*
a piece of	*ein Stück*
to appear	*auftauchen, erscheinen*
apple	*Apfel*
application	*Bewerbung*
appointment	*Termin*
appreciated	*geschätzt*
apprentice	*Auszubildende/r*
apprenticeship	*Ausbildung*
April	*April*
archaeology	*Archäologie*
area	*Gebiet, Gegend*
Argentina	*Argentinien*
to argue	*argumentieren, streiten*
arm	*Arm*
armchair	*Sessel*
around	*herum*
to arrange	*planen*
arrival	*Ankunft*
to arrive	*ankommen*
art	*Kunst*
article	*Artikel*

artist	*Künstler/in*
as ... as	*so ... wie*
as a matter of fact	*tatsächlich, in der Tat*
to ask	*fragen*
to ask for	*fragen nach, bitten um*
to ask sb out	*jdmn einladen, sich mit jmdm verabreden*
at	*an, bei, um*
at night	*nachts*
attached	*im Anhang (E-Mail)*
to attend	*besuchen, beiwohnen*
attention	*Aufmerksamkeit*
at the same time	*gleichzeitig*
attic	*Speicher, Dachboden*
attractive	*attraktiv*
August	*August*
Australia	*Australien*
Austria	*Österreich*
autumn	*Herbst*
available	*verfügbar*
awake	*wach*
away	*weg*
awfully	*außerordentlich, furchtbar*
a while	*eine Weile*

B

baby	*Baby*
baby bottle	*Babyfläschchen*
back	*zurück*
back	*Rücken*
backache	*Rückenschmerzen*
back stairs	*Hintertreppe*
back up	*zurück nach oben*
backpack (AE)	*Rucksack*
backstreet	*Seitensträßchen*
backyard	*Garten hinter dem Haus*
bacon	*Speck, Bacon*
bad	*schlecht*
bag	*Tasche*
baggage	*Gepäck*
balance	*Gleichgewicht*
balcony	*Balkon*
bald	*kahl, glatzköpfig*
balloon	*Ballon*
bank	*Bank*
bank clerk	*Bankangestellte/r*
banner	*Banner, Transparent*
bar	*Gitterstab; Bar*
basement	*Keller*
basketball	*Basketball*
to bathe	*baden*
bathroom	*Badezimmer*
bathtub	*Badewanne*
to be about to do sth.	*gerade etw. tun wollen*
beard	*Bart*
to be arrested	*verhaftet werden*
to beat	*schlagen*
to be back	*zurück sein*
to be called	*heißen*
Be careful!	*Sei/Seien Sie vorsichtig!*
to be determined	*entschlossen sein*
to be divorced	*geschieden sein*
to be engaged	*verlobt sein*
to be joking	*einen Scherz machen*
to be late	*sich verspäten*
to be lost	*sich verirrt haben*
to be scared	*Angst haben*
to be sure	*sicher sein*
to be tired of doing sth.	*keine Lust mehr haben, etw. zu tun*
beautiful	*(wunder)schön*
because	*weil*
because of	*wegen*
to become	*werden*
bed	*Bett*
bed and breakfast	*Pension*
bedroom	*Schlafzimmer*
beer	*Bier*
before	*vor(her)*
to begin	*anfangen*
behind	*hinter; Hintern (Gesäß)*
believe	*glauben*
belly	*Magen, Bauch*
to belong to	*gehören*
belongings (pl.)	*Besitztümer, Habseligkeiten*
beloved	*geliebt*
below	*darunter*
bench	*Bank*
beside	*neben*
best	*beste/r/s*
better	*besser/e/r/s*
between	*zwischen*
beverage	*Getränk*
bicycle	*Fahrrad*
big	*groß*
bike	*Fahrrad*
bill	*Rechnung*
billion	*Milliarde*
bin (AE)	*Mülleimer*
bird	*Vogel*
birth	*Geburt*
birthday	*Geburtstag*
biscuit (BE)	*Keks*
a bit	*ein bisschen*
bit	*Stückchen*
black	*schwarz*
blanket	*Decke*
blazer	*Blazer, Jackett*
blonde	*blond*
blood	*Blut*
blouse	*Bluse*
blue	*blau*
to blush	*erröten*
boat	*Boot*
to boil	*kochen (Wasser)*
book	*Buch*
to book	*buchen*
booking	*Buchung*
boot	*Stiefel*

boring	*langweilig*
born	*geboren*
both	*beide*
bottle	*Flasche*
bottom	*Boden, Grund; Gesäß*
bouquet	*Blumenstrauß*
boutique	*Boutique, Modegeschäft*
bowl	*Schüssel*
box	*Schachtel; Kiste*
boy	*Junge*
boyfriend	*Freund*
branch	*Niederlassung*
brave	*tapfer, mutig*
Brazil	*Brasilien*
bread	*Brot*
to break	*(zer)brechen, kaputtgehen*
breakfast	*Frühstück*
breath	*Atem*
breathtaking	*atemberaubend*
breeze	*Brise*
bridge	*Brücke*
brief	*kurz*
bright	*hell, strahlend*
to bring (along)	*mitbringen*
British	*britisch, Brite, Britin*
brochure	*Prospekt*
broken	*kaputt*
brother	*Bruder*
brown	*braun*
to brush one's teeth	*sich die Zähne putzen*
buddy	*Kumpel, Freund, Freundchen*
budget	*Budget*
to build	*bauen*
bus	*Bus*
business	*Geschäft, Betrieb*
business people	*Geschäftsleute*
business woman	*Geschäftsfrau*
busy	*beschäftigt*
but	*aber*
butcher	*Metzger*
butter	*Butter*
to buy	*kaufen*
by	*neben, bei; bis*
bye	*Tschüss*
by now	*inzwischen*
by the way	*übrigens*

C

cab driver	*Taxifahrer/in*
cake	*Kuchen; Torte*
call	*Anruf*
to call	*anrufen*
to call it a day	*Feierabend machen*
calmly	*ruhig, gelassen*
camera	*Kamera*
can	*können*
Canada	*Kanada*
Canadian	*kanadisch, Kanadier/in*
candle	*Kerze*
can't stand sth	*etw. nicht aushalten zu können*
canyon	*Schlucht*
cap	*Mütze*
capital	*Hauptstadt*
captain	*Kapitän*
to capture a moment	*den Moment festhalten*
car	*Auto*
caravan	*Wohnwagen*
to care about sb./sth.	*sich um jdn./etw. kümmern, sich sorgen*
careful	*vorsichtig*
carpenter	*Zimmermann, Schreiner/in*
carrot	*Möhre*
to carry	*tragen*
case	*Fall*
castle	*Burg, Schloss*
casual	*locker; Freizeit-*
catch	*Fang*
to catch one's breath	*Atem holen*
to celebrate	*feiern*
cellar	*Keller*
centre	*Mitte*
certainly	*sicherlich*
chair	*Stuhl*
challenge	*Herausforderung*
champagne	*Champagner; Sekt*
change	*Wechsel, Veränderung*
to change	*sich verändern*
to change trains	*umsteigen*
to chase	*jagen*
cheap	*billig, günstig*
to check	*überprüfen, kontrollieren, checken*
to check in	*einchecken*
to check sth out	*sich etw. anschauen*
cheerful	*fröhlich*
Cheers!	*Prost; Danke*
to cheer sb up	*jmdn aufmuntern*
cheese	*Käse*
chef	*Chefkoch*
chemist's	*Apotheke*
chemistry	*Chemie*
cherry	*Kirsche*
chest	*Brust*
chicken	*Hähnchen*
child (pl. children)	*Kind*
children's room	*Kinderzimmer*
Chile	*Chile*
China	*China; Porzellan*
Chinese	*chinesisch, Chinese, Chinesin*
chocolate	*Schokolade*
choice	*Wahl*
to choke	*würgen*
to choose	*(aus)wählen*
Christmas	*Weihnachten*
church	*Kirche*

cigarette	*Zigarette*
cinema	*Kino*
circus	*Zirkus*
city	*Stadt*
city map	*Stadtplan*
class	*Klasse, Kurs*
classmate	*Klassenkamerad, Mitschüler/in*
clean	*sauber*
to clean	*putzen, aufräumen*
clear	*klar*
clearly	*klar*
clever	*schlau, klug*
client	*Kunde/Kundin, Auftraggeber/in*
cliff	*Felsen, Klippe*
to climb (up)	*(hinauf-)klettern*
clock	*Uhr*
to close	*schließen*
close	*nahe*
closet	*Garderobe, Abstellkammer*
clothes (pl.)	*Kleidung*
cloud	*Wolke*
cloudy	*wolkig*
coach	*Reisebus*
coast	*Küste*
coat	*Mantel*
coat rack	*Garderobe*
coffee	*Kaffee*
cold	*kalt*
cold	*Erkältung*
colleague	*Kollege, Kollegin*
college	*(BE) Schule; (AE) Universität*
colour	*Farbe*
colourful	*bunt, farbenfroh*
to come	*kommen*
to come from	*kommen von/aus*
Come on!	*Komm(t)! Auf geht's!*
comfortable	*bequem*
commercial	*Werbung, Werbespot*
compartment	*Zugabteil*
to complete	*vervollständigen*
completely	*völlig, total*
compliment	*Kompliment*
computer	*Rechner*
computer science	*Informatik*
to concentrate	*sich konzentrieren*
to concern sb	*jmdn beunruhigen*
concert	*Konzert*
cone	*Waffel (Eis)*
confused	*verwirrt*
connection	*Verbindung, Beziehung*
to consider	*erwägen, etw. überlegen*
consideration	*Berücksichtigung*
to consist of	*bestehen aus*
constantly	*ständig*
to consult sth	*in etw. nachschlagen*
to consume	*verzehren, essen*
to continue	*weitermachen*
contract	*Vertrag*
conversation	*Gespräch*
convertible	*Kabrio*
to cook	*kochen*
cookout (AE)	*Grillparty*
cool	*kühl*
to copy	*kopieren*
correct	*richtig*
corridor	*Flur, Gang*
to cost	*kosten*
cottage	*Cottage (kleines Landhaus)*
couch	*Couch*
to cough	*husten*
cough syrup	*Hustensaft*
could	*könnte, konnte*
counter	*Theke*
country	*Land*
countryside	*Landschaft*
couple	*Paar, Pärchen*
to cover	*bedecken*
cover	*Schicht, Decke*
crazy	*verrückt*
cream	*Sahne, Creme*
Crete	*Kreta*
to cross	*überqueren*
crossroads	*Kreuzung*
crossword	*Kreuzworträtsel*
crowd	*Menschenmenge*
cruise	*Kreuzfahrt*
to cry	*rufen; weinen*
Cuba	*Kuba*
cucumber	*Gurke*
cuisine	*Küche (Essen)*
culture	*Kultur*
cup	*Tasse*
curiously	*neugierig*
curly	*lockig, kraushaarig*
curtain	*Vorhang, Gardinen*
customer	*Kunde*
to cut	*schneiden*
cutting board	*Schneidebrett*
to cycle	*Fahrrad fahren*
Czech	*tschechisch; Tscheche, Tschechin*

D

daft (BE)	*dumm, blöd*
dairy products	*Milchprodukte*
dance	*tanzen*
dangerous	*gefährlich*
to dare	*sich trauen*
dark	*dunkel*
darkness	*Dunkelheit*
darling	*Liebling, Süße*
date	*Datum; Date, Verabredung*
date of birth	*Geburtsdatum*
daughter	*Tochter*
day	*Tag*

day after tomorrow	*übermorgen*
day before yesterday	*vorgestern*
day trip	*Tagesausflug*
dear	*liebe/r/s*
dear God	*Gott im Himmel, Herrgott*
decade	*Jahrzehnt*
December	*Dezember*
to decide	*entscheiden*
decision	*Entscheidung*
deep	*tief*
degree	*Hochschulabschluss*
delicious	*lecker, köstlich*
Denmark	*Dänemark*
dentist	*Zahnarzt*
department store	*Kaufhaus*
to describe	*beschreiben*
desert	*Wüste*
desk	*Schreibtisch*
despite	*trotz*
detail	*Detail, Einzelheit*
determined	*entschlossen*
to develop	*entwickeln*
to die	*sterben*
difficult	*schwierig*
dinner	*Abendessen*
direction	*Richtung*
director of sales	*Verkaufsleiter*
direct	*direkt*
directly	*direkt*
dirt	*Dreck*
dirty	*schmutzig*
disappointed	*enttäuscht*
to discover	*entdecken*
to discuss	*besprechen*
disease	*Krankheit*
dishes	*Geschirr; Gerichte*
display	*Bildschirm*
distance	*Entfernung*
distant	*entfernt*
to distract	*ablenken*
distraction	*Ablenkung*
to disturb	*stören*
to dive	*tauchen*
divorced	*geschieden*
dizzy	*schwindelig*
to do	*tun*
to do the dishes	*den Abwasch machen*
doctor	*Doktor, Arzt*
don't panic!	*Nur keine Panik!*
don't worry	*das macht nichts*
door	*Tür*
dot	*Punkt*
double	*doppelt*
double room	*Doppelzimmer*
down	*hinunter, nach unten*
downer	*Spielverderber/in*
dream	*Traum*
dress	*Kleid*
dresser	*Kommode*
to drink	*trinken*
drink	*Getränk*
to drive	*fahren (mit dem Auto)*
driver	*Fahrer/in*
dry	*trocken*
due to	*infolge, wegen*
duffel bag	*Seesack*
dull	*langweilig, uninteressant*
dumb (AE)	*dumm*
during	*während*
dust	*Staub*
Dutch	*niederländisch*

E

each other	*einander*
ear	*Ohr*
earlier	*früher*
early	*früh*
to earn	*verdienen*
to ease	*lindern; erleichtern*
easily	*leicht*
east	*östlich, nach Osten*
East	*Osten*
easy	*leicht*
to eat	*essen*
economics	*Wirtschaft, Ökonomie*
edge	*Rand*
egg	*Ei*
eight	*acht*
eighth	*der/ die / das achte*
eighty	*achtzig*
elderly	*älter/e/r/s, Senioren-*
elegant	*elegant*
elevator	*Lift, Aufzug*
else	*(sonst) noch*
email	*E-Mail*
to embrace	*umarmen*
emergency	*Notfall*
to emphasize	*betonen*
empty	*leer*
energy	*Energie*
engagement	*Verlobung*
engine	*Maschine, Motor*
England	*England*
English	*englisch; Engländer/in*
English Channel	*Ärmelkanal*
to enjoy	*genießen*
enough	*genug*
to enter	*eintreten; eingeben (Computer)*
even	*sogar*
even though	*obwohl*
evening	*Abend*
event	*Ereignis*
every	*jede/r/s*
everybody	*jede/r/s*
everything	*alles*
exactly	*genau*
exam	*Prüfung, Klausur*
to exceed	*übersteigen*
excellent	*hervorragend, ausgezeichnet*

excited	*aufgeregt*
exciting	*aufregend, spannend*
Excuse me!	*Entschuldigung!, Entschuldigen Sie bitte/ Entschuldige bitte, ...!*
to exercise	*trainieren, Sport machen*
exhibition	*Ausstellung*
to exit	*hinausgehen*
exotic	*exotisch*
to expect	*erwarten*
expensive	*teuer*
to experience	*(mit)erleben*
experiment	*Experiment*
expert	*Experte, Expertin*
to explain	*erklären*
to explore	*erkunden*
expression	*Ausdruck*
eye	*Auge*

F

fabulous	*fabelhaft*
face	*Gesicht*
fact	*Tatsache*
fake	*erfunden, falsch*
fair	*Messe*
fall	*Herbst*
to fall	*fallen*
to fall asleep	*einschlafen*
fame	*Ruhm*
familiar	*bekannt*
family	*Familie*
famous	*berühmt*
fantastic	*fantastisch*
far	*weit*
faraway	*fern*
far too	*viel zu*
farm	*Bauernhof*
fascinating	*faszinierend*
fashion	*Mode*
fast	*schnell*
fat	*dick, fett*
father	*Vater*
fault	*Fehler*
favourite	*Lieblings-*
February	*Februar*
to feed	*füttern*
to feel	*(sich) fühlen*
to feel like doing sth	*Lust auf etw. zu tun zu haben*
to feel sick	*sich schlecht fühlen, jdm. ist schlecht*
to feel sorry for sb.	*Mitleid mit jdm. haben*
female	*weiblich/e/r/s*
fence	*Zaun*
fever	*Fieber*
a few	*ein paar*
field	*Feld, Bereich*
fifth	*der / die / das fünfte*
fifty	*fünfzig*
figure	*Gestalt*
file	*Datei*
to fill sth. in	*etw. ausfüllen*
final	*letzte/r/s, End-*
finally	*schließlich*
finance	*Finanzwesen*
to find	*finden*
to find out	*herausfinden*
fine	*gut*
finger	*Finger*
to finish	*beenden*
to fire up (AE)	*etw. anzünden*
first	*zuerst; erste/r/s*
first name	*Vorname*
fish	*Fisch*
fish and chips	*Fisch und Pommes Frites*
to fit	*passen*
five	*fünf*
to fix	*reparieren*
to flash	*blinken*
flat	*flach; Wohnung*
flight	*Flug*
to flip through	*durchblättern*
flood	*Überflutung*
floor	*Stockwerk; Boden*
floorlamp	*Stehlampe*
flower	*Blume*
to fly	*fliegen*
folks	*Leute (informell)*
to follow	*folgen*
food	*Essen*
fool	*Idiot*
foot (pl: feet)	*Fuß (auch Längenmaß, ca. 30 cm)*
football	*Fußball*
for	*für; seit*
for a moment	*einen Augenblick lang*
forest	*Wald*
to forget	*vergessen*
fork	*Gabel*
formal	*formell*
former	*ehemalige/r/s*
forty	*vierzig*
forward(s)	*vorwärts, nach vorn*
four	*vier*
fourth	*der/ die / das vierte*
France	*Frankreich*
free	*kostenlos*
French	*französisch; Franzose(n)*
frequent flyer miles	*Bonusmeilen*
frequently	*häufig, regelmäßig, oft*
Friday	*Freitag*
fridge	*Kühlschrank*
fried	*frittiert, gebraten*
friend	*Freund/in*
friendly	*freundlich*
fries (AE)	*Pommes Frites*
from	*von, aus*
front desk	*Empfang; Rezeption (Hotel)*
fruit	*Obst*
frustrated	*frustriert*

to fry	*braten*
full	*voll; satt*
fun	*Spaß*
funny	*lustig, seltsam*
fur	*Pelz*
furniture	*Möbel*
future	*Zukunft*

G

game	*Spiel*
garage	*Garage, Autowerkstatt*
garbage (AE)	*Abfall*
garden	*Garten*
garlic	*Knoblauch*
gas	*(AE) Benzin, Sprit; Kohlensäure (Wasser)*
geography	*Geografie*
German	*deutsch; Deutsche/r*
Germany	*Deutschland*
to get	*erreichen, bekommen; werden*
to get a signal	*Empfang haben*
to get divorced	*sich scheiden lassen*
to get dressed	*sich anziehen*
to get engaged	*sich verloben*
to get hold of sth.	*etwas zu fassen bekommen*
to get sb. back to	*jdn. zurückbringen*
to get to know sb.	*jdn. kennenlernen*
to get to sth.	*etw. erreichen*
to get up	*aufstehen*
gift	*Geschenk*
gift certificate	*Gutschein*
girl	*Mädchen*
girlfriend	*Freundin*
to give sth. to so.	*jdm. etw. geben*
glass	*Glas*
glasses (pl.)	*Brille*
to go	*gehen*
to go on	*weitermachen*
to go out	*ausgehen*
gold	*golden*
good	*gut*
good-looking	*gutaussehend*
Good afternoon!	*Guten Tag!*
Good evening!	*Guten Abend!*
Good morning!	*Guten Morgen!*
Good night!	*Gute Nacht!*
gorgeous	*wunderschön*
gown	*Talar, Richterrobe; Kleid*
to grab	*packen*
grade (AE)	*Note*
to graduate	*absolvieren*
graduation	*(Hoch-)Schulabschluss(-feier)*
grandfather	*Großvater*
grandmother	*Großmutter*
grand opening	*feierliche Eröffnung*
grass	*Gras*
great	*groß, großartig, toll*
Great Britain	*Großbritannien*
Greece	*Griechenland*
green	*grün*
greencard	*Niederlassungserlaubnis (USA)*
greengrocer	*Gemüsehändler/-in*
grey	*grau*
groceries	*Lebensmittel(einkäufe)*
grocery store	*Lebensmittelgeschäft*
ground	*Erde, Boden*
ground floor	*Erdgeschoss*
group	*Gruppe*
to guess	*raten*
guest	*Gast*
guidebook	*Reiseführer (Buch)*
guilty	*schuldig*
guitar	*Guitarre*
guy	*Typ, Kerl*
gym	*Fitnessstudio*

H

hair	*Haar(e)*
hair dresser	*Friseur/in*
hair stylist	*Friseur/in*
half	*halb, Hälfte*
hall	*Eingangshalle, Flur*
hallway	*Flur*
ham	*Schinken*
hammer	*Hammer*
hand	*Hand*
handsome	*gutaussehend (Mann)*
to hang up	*aufhängen*
to happen	*geschehen, passieren*
happy	*glücklich, froh*
hard	*hart, schwierig*
hardly	*kaum*
hat	*Hut*
to hate	*hassen*
to have	*haben*
to have a baby	*ein Kind bekommen*
to have a go	*etw. versuchen*
to have a look at sth.	*etwas anschauen*
Have a nice day!	*Schönen Tag noch!*
to have sth in mind	*etw. vorhaben*
to have to	*müssen*
he	*er*
head	*Kopf*
to head home	*nach Hause gehen*
to head off to sth	*sich auf dem Weg machen nach*
healthy	*gesund*
to hear	*hören*
heart	*Herz*
heart attack	*Herzinfarkt*
heaven	*Himmel*
heavy	*schwer*
height	*Höhe*
hello	*Hallo*
to help	*helfen*
to help out	*aushelfen*
helpful	*hilfsbereit*

her	*ihr; ihr/e*
here	*hier*
hereby	*hiermit*
here we go	*los geht's*
here you are	*bitte schön*
high	*hoch*
high school	*Highschool*
to hike	*wandern*
hiking boots	*Wanderschuhe*
hill	*Hügel*
him	*ihn, ihm*
his	*sein/e*
history	*Geschichte*
to hit	*treffen, hier: überfahren*
hobby (pl. hobbies)	*Hobby*
to hold	*halten*
holiday	*Urlaub; Feiertag*
home	*Zuhause*
homework	*Hausaufgabe*
honey	*Honig; Liebling, Süße*
to hope	*hoffen*
hopeful	*hoffnungsvoll*
hopefully	*hoffentlich*
horrible	*schrecklich*
hospital	*Krankenhaus*
hot	*heiß*
hotel	*Hotel*
hotel room	*Hotelzimmer*
hour	*Stunde*
house	*Haus*
housework	*Hausarbeit*
how	*wie*
however	*aber, jedoch*
to hug	*umarmen*
huge	*groß, hier: breit*
hundred	*Hundert*
Hungary	*Ungarn*
hungry	*hungrig*
to hurry up	*sich beeilen*
to hurt	*verletzen; schmerzen*
husband	*Ehemann*

I

I	*ich*
ice cream	*Eiscreme*
ice cream parlour	*Eisdiele*
I do love	*ich mag ... sehr*
I'm sorry	*Entschuldigung!, Entschuldigen Sie bitte/ Entschuldige bitte, ...!*
idea	*Idee, Ahnung*
if	*wenn, falls*
if you say so...	*wenn du meinst ...*
to imagine	*sich etw. vorstellen*
immediately	*sofort*
important	*wichtig*
impossible	*unmöglich*
impressed	*beeindruckt*
impressive	*beeindruckend, eindrucksvoll*
in	*in*
in a hurry	*in Eile*
in charge of	*für etw. zuständig sein*
to include	*beinhalten*
inexpensive	*günstig*
in fact	*eigentlich*
in favour of	*für etw. sein*
information	*Informationen, Auskunft*
in front of	*vor (räumlich)*
inch	*Zoll (2,54 cm)*
incredibly	*unglaublich*
indeed	*tatsächlich*
India	*Indien*
indicator	*Blinker*
industries	*Industrien*
infant	*Baby*
in front of	*vor*
ingredient	*Zutat*
injured	*verletzt*
injury	*Verletzung*
in love	*verliebt*
innocent	*unschuldig*
to inquire	*nachfragen*
insane	*verrückt*
inside	*innen (drin)*
instead (of)	*stattdessen, anstatt (von)*
insurance	*Versicherung*
intelligent	*intelligent*
intention	*Absicht*
to interest	*interessieren*
interesting	*interessant*
into	*in (hinein)*
to introduce	*vorstellen (jdm.); (neu) einführen*
invention	*Erfindung*
invitation	*Einladung*
to invite	*einladen*
Iranian	*iranisch, Iranier/in*
Ireland	*Irland*
Irish	*irisch; Ire/in*
iron	*(Bügel-)Eisen*
to iron	*bügeln*
irresistable	*unwiderstehlich*
island	*Insel*
it	*es; ihm*
it doesn't matter	*das macht nichts*
it's fine	*es macht nichts, es ist in Ordnung*
Italian	*italienisch; Italiener/in*
Italy	*Italien*

J

jacket	*Jacke*
jam	*Marmelade*
January	*Januar*
Japan	*Japan*
Japanese	*japanisch, Japaner/in*
jar	*Glas*
(a pair of) jeans	*Jeans*
jewellery	*Schmuck*
job	*Arbeit(sstelle)*

to jog	*joggen*
to join sb.	*jmd. Gesellschaft leisten*
to joke	*scherzen*
journalist	*Journalist/in*
journey	*Reise*
joyful	*freudig*
judge	*Richter/in*
to juggle	*mehrere Sachen gleichzeitig machen*
juice	*Saft*
July	*Juli*
to jump	*springen*
jumper	*Pulli*
to jump in	*hineinspringen*
June	*Juni*
junk	*Schrott*
just	*nur; gerade eben*
Just do it!	*Mach(t)'s einfach!*
just like that	*einfach so*

K

to keep	*behalten; bewahren*
Keep the change!	*Stimmt so!*
key	*Schlüssel*
keyboard	*Tastatur*
keycard	*Schlüsselkarte (im Hotel)*
keypad	*Tastatur*
kid	*Kind*
to kill	*töten*
kind	*nett*
kitchen	*Küche*
knee	*Knie*
knife (pl: knives)	*Messer*
to knock	*klopfen*
to know	*wissen, kennen*

L

laboratory	*Labor*
lady	*Dame*
lake	*See*
lamp	*Lampe*
to land	*landen*
language	*Sprache*
laptop	*Notebook*
large	*groß*
last	*letzte/r/s*
last name	*Nachname*
late	*(zu) spät*
later	*später*
to laugh	*lachen*
laughter	*Gelächter*
law	*Recht, Jura*
lawyer	*Anwalt, Anwältin*
to lead	*hinführen*
to learn	*lernen*
to leave	*verlassen*
lecture	*Vorlesung*
lecture hall	*Hörsaal*
left	*(nach) links*
leg	*Bein*
lemon	*Zitrone*
lemonade	*Zitronenbrause*
less	*weniger*
to let sb. in	*jdn. hereinlassen*
lettuce	*Salat*
to lie	*liegen*
life	*Leben*
lift	*Lift, Aufzug*
to lift	*heben*
light	*hell; Licht*
to light	*beleuchten; anzünden (Kerzen)*
lightning	*Blitz*
to like	*mögen, gern haben*
like	*wie*
line	*Linie; Schlange*
link	*Link*
litre	*Liter*
list	*Liste*
to listen	*zuhören*
little	*klein, wenig*
little more than	*wenig mehr als*
to live	*leben, wohnen*
living	*Lebensunterhalt*
living room	*Wohnzimmer*
lobby	*Eingangsbereich, Lobby*
local	*örtlich, aus der Gegend*
location	*Platz, Ort*
to log in	*einloggen*
London	*London*
long	*lang*
long-distance relationship	*Fernbeziehung*
to look	*gucken; aussehen*
to look at sb.	*jdn. anschauen*
to look back	*zurückschauen*
to look best	*am besten aussehen*
to look for sth./sb.	*jdn./etw. suchen*
to look forward to sth.	*sich freuen auf etw.*
to look fun	*etw. sieht lustig aus*
to look over one's shoulder	*über die/jds. Schulter schauen*
loose	*locker, weit*
to lose sth./sb.	*etw./jdn. verlieren*
to lose track of sth	*den Überblick von etw. verlieren*
loss	*Verlust*
lost	*verloren*
a lot	*viel*
loud	*laut*
love	*Liebe*
to love	*lieben*
to love to do sth.	*etwas sehr gerne tun*
loveable	*liebenswert*
lovely	*hübsch*
low	*niedrig*
luck	*Glück*
luckily	*glücklicherweise*
lunch	*Mittagessen*

M

magazine	*Zeitschrift, Illustrierte*
to maintain	*pflegen, aufrechterhalten*
major (subject)	*Hauptfach*
to make it somewhere	*es irgendwo schaffen*
to make oneself comfortable	*es sich bequem machen*
to make sense	*sinnvoll sein*
to make s.o. do s.t.	*jdn. dazu veranlassen etw. zu tun*
to make s.o. feel tired	*jmd. müde werden lassen*
to make sure	*sich vergewissern*
Malta	*Malta*
Maltese	*maltesisch; Malteser/in*
man	*Mann*
to manage	*etw einrichten können; zurecht kommen können*
to manipulate	*manipulieren*
many	*viele*
map	*Landkarte*
mark (BE)	*Note*
marital status	*Familienstand*
March	*März*
market	*Markt*
marketplace	*Marktplatz*
marriage	*Ehe*
married	*verheiratet*
to marry	*heiraten*
massive	*riesengroß*
to matter	*ausmachen*
May	*Mai*
may	*dürfen*
maybe	*vielleicht*
me	*mich, mir*
meadow	*Wiese*
meal	*Gericht*
to mean	*meinen*
meat	*Fleisch*
mechanic	*Mechaniker/in*
medication	*Medikament*
medicine	*Medizin*
to meet (up with) sb	*jmdn treffen*
meeting	*Konferenz; Treffen*
memory	*Erinnerung; Gedächtnis*
to mention	*erwähnen*
menu	*Karte, Menü*
mess	*Durcheinander*
message	*Nachricht*
messy	*unordentlich*
Mexico	*Mexiko*
middle	*Mitte, mitten (in)*
midnight	*Mitternacht*
mitten	*Fäustling*
motorway	*Autobahn*
might	*könnte (vielleicht)*
mile	*Meile (1,6 km)*
milk	*Milch*
million	*Million*
minced meat	*Hackfleisch*
to mind	*aufpassen auf, beachten; sich kümmern*
mint	*Minze*
minute	*Minute*
mirror	*Spiegel*
to mix together	*sich vermischen*
mixture	*Mischung*
mobile phone	*Mobiltelefon, Handy*
moment	*Moment*
Monday	*Montag*
money	*Geld*
month	*Monat*
moon	*Mond*
more	*mehr*
morning	*Morgen*
most	*meist/e/r/s*
mother	*Mutter*
mountain	*Berg*
mountain biker	*Mountainbikefahrer/in*
mouse	*Maus*
mouth	*Mund*
to move	*(sich) bewegen; umziehen*
movie	*(Kino-)Film*
much	*viel*
mud	*Schlamm*
muddy	*schlammig*
multiple	*viele*
Mum (BE)	*Mama, Mutti*
to mumble	*grummeln*
muscular	*muskulös*
mushroom	*Champignon, Pilz*
music	*Musik*
must	*müssen*
to mutter	*murmeln*
my	*mein/e*
my God	*mein Gott*

N

nail	*Nagel*
name	*Name*
nap	*Nickerchen*
napkin	*Serviette*
narrow	*eng*
nationality	*Nationalität*
nauseous	*übel*
near	*nahe, in der Nähe*
nearly	*fast*
neat	*ordentlich, hübsch*
neck	*Hals*
need	*Bedürfnis*
to need	*müssen, brauchen*
nephew	*Neffe*
nervous	*nervös*
never	*niemals*
never even	*noch überhaupt nicht*
never mind	*macht nichts, ist doch egal; vergiss es*
new	*neu*
newborn	*Neugeborenes*
newly	*neu*

	news	*Nachrichten*
	news headlines	*Schlagzeilen*
	newspaper	*Zeitung*
	New Zealand	*Neuseeland*
	next	*nächste/r/s*
	next to	*neben*
	nice	*nett*
	niece	*Nichte*
	night	*Nacht*
	nightmare	*Alptraum*
	nine	*neun*
	ninth	*der/ die / das neunte*
	ninety	*neunzig*
	nobody	*niemand*
	normally	*normalerweise*
	no more than	*nicht mehr als*
	no one	*niemand*
	no problem	*kein Problem*
	no worries	*Keine Sorge!*
	nonsense	*Quatsch, Unsinn*
	noon	*Mittag*
	normal	*normal*
	north	*nördlich, nach Norden*
	North	*Norden*
	Northern Ireland	*Nordirland*
	Norway	*Norwegen*
	Norwegian	*norwegisch, Norweger/in*
	nose	*Nase*
	not ... even	*nicht einmal*
	note	*Notiz*
	nothing	*nichts*
to	notice	*bemerken*
	November	*November*
	now	*jetzt*
	nowhere	*nirgendwo*
	number	*Nummer*
	nurse	*Pfleger(in)*

O

	o'clock	*Uhr (Zeitangabe)*
	occasion	*Gelegenheit*
	occasionally	*gelegentlich*
	occupation	*Beruf*
	October	*Oktober*
	of	*von*
	of course	*natürlich*
	offer	*Angebot*
to	offer	*anbieten*
	office	*Büro*
	often	*oft, häufig*
	ointment	*Salbe*
	old	*alt*
	on	*auf; an, am*
	once more	*noch einmal*
	one	*eine/r/s*
	onion	*Zwiebel*
	only	*nur*
	on time	*pünktlich*
	onto	*auf ... hinauf*
to	open	*öffnen*
to	open up	*eröffnen*
	opinion	*Meinung*
	opposite	*gegenüber*
	optician	*Optiker/in*
	or	*oder*
	ordinary	*gewöhnlich*
to	organise	*organisieren*
	originally	*ursprünglich*
	other	*andere/r/s*
	out	*hinaus*
	out here/there	*hier/dort draußen*
	outlet	*Steckdose*
	out of fashion	*altmodisch*
	outside	*außen, draußen*
	oven	*Ofen*
	over	*über*
	overseas	*Übersee...; Auslands...*
to	overwhelm sb (with sth)	*jmdn mit etw. überschütten*
	own	*eigene/r/s*
	owner	*Eigentümer/in*

P

	p.m.	*Nachmittag; Abend*
to	pack	*packen*
	pack	*Packung*
	package	*Packung; Paket*
	page	*Seite*
	pain	*Schmerz*
to	paint	*malen*
	painter	*Maler/-in*
	a pair of	*ein Paar*
	palace	*Palast, Schloss*
	pan	*Pfanne*
	pancake	*Pfannkuchen*
to	panic	*in Panik geraten*
	parents (Pl.)	*Eltern*
	park	*Park*
	parking space	*Parkplatz*
	part	*Teil*
to	pass	*bestehen (Prüfung)*
	passenger seat	*Beifahrersitz*
	password	*Passwort*
	past	*nach (zeitlich); vorbei an*
	path	*Pfad*
	patient	*Patient*
to	pay	*bezahlen*
to	pay attention to sb/sth	*auf jmdn./etw. aufpassen*
	pedestrian	*Fußgänger/in*
	pedestrian zone	*Fußgängerzone*
to	peel	*schälen*
	pensioner	*Rentner/-in*
	people	*Leute, Menschen*
	peoples (Pl.)	*Völker*
	pepper	*Pfeffer*
	perfect	*perfekt*
	perfectly	*hier: völlig; perfekt*
	perfume	*Parfüm*
	permanently	*permanent*

personal	*persönlich*
phone	*Telefon, Handy*
to phone sb.	*jdn. anrufen*
photography	*Fotografie*
physics	*Physik*
piano	*Klavier*
to pick	*auswählen*
to pick sth up	*etw. abholen; etw. aufheben*
picture	*Bild*
picturesque	*malerisch*
piece	*Stück*
pill	*Tablette, Pille*
pillow	*Kissen*
pink	*pink, rosa*
to pitch an idea	*eine Idee einbringen*
place	*Platz; Ort; Wohnung*
place of resisdence	*Wohnort*
plain	*einfach, schlicht*
plan	*Plan*
to plan	*planen*
plane	*Flugzeug*
to plaster	*pflastern*
plastic	*Plastik*
plate	*Teller*
platform	*Gleis*
to play	*spielen*
please	*bitte*
Please be seated!	*Bitte nehmen Sie Platz!*
pleasure	*Vergnügen*
plenty of	*viel*
plug	*Stecker*
pocket	*Tasche (an Kleidungsstück)*
pocket money	*Taschengeld*
poetry	*Dichtung, Poesie*
to point to	*zeigen auf*
Poland	*Polen*
policeman/-woman	*Polizist/-in*
Polish	*polnisch*
polite	*höflich*
polo shirt	*Poloshirt*
Portugal	*Portugal*
Portuguese	*Portugiese, Portugiesin; portugiesisch*
position	*Stelle*
positive	*positiv*
possible	*möglich*
possibly	*vermutlich*
to post	*posten (elektronische Nachrichten, Bilder)*
post office	*Postamt*
pot	*Topf*
potato	*Kartoffel*
pound	*Pfund*
to pour	*einschenken*
to practice	*üben*
pregnant	*schwanger*
to prepare	*vorbereiten*
prepared	*bereit, vorbereitet*
to prescribe	*verschreiben*
prescription	*Arztrezept*
present	*Geschenk*
to press	*drücken*
to pretend	*vorgeben*
pretty	*hübsch*
price	*Preis*
princess	*Prinzessin*
to print	*drucken*
printer	*Drucker*
prison	*Gefängnis*
probably	*wahrscheinlich*
problem	*Problem*
product	*Produkt*
profession	*Beruf*
program(me)	*Programm*
project	*Projekt*
promise	*Versprechen*
to promise	*versprechen*
promotion	*Beförderung*
proof	*Beweis*
proud	*stolz*
pub	*Kneipe*
Puerto Rico	*Puerto Rico*
to pull	*ziehen*
to pull one's hand away	*seine Hand wegziehen*
to pull s.o. up	*jdn. hochziehen*
purple	*violett*
purse	*Handtasche*
to push sth. open	*aufdrücken*
to put	*setzen, stellen, legen*
to put on makeup	*sich schminken*
to put together	*zusammensetzen*

Q

queen	*Königin*
queue	*Schlange*
to queue	*Schlange stehen*
question	*Frage*
quick	*schnell*
quickly	*schnell*
quiet	*ruhig, still*
quite	*ziemlich*

R

radiator	*Heizkörper*
radio	*Radio*
rain	*Regen*
rainy	*regnerisch*
rarely	*selten, kaum*
to reach	*erreichen*
to read	*lesen*
reading	*Lesung*
ready	*bereit*
real	*echt*
to realise	*bemerken*
reality	*Wirklichkeit*
really	*wirklich, echt, sehr*
to receive	*erhalten, bekommen, empfangen*
recently	*kürzlich*

reception	*Empfang, Rezeption*
receptionist	*Empfangsmitarbeiter/in, Rezeptionist/in*
recipe	*Rezept*
to record	*aufnehmen*
red	*rot*
refrigerator	*Kühlschrank*
relationship	*Beziehung*
to relax	*entspannen*
relief	*Linderung; Erleichterung*
religion	*Religion*
to remember	*sich erinnern an*
remote control	*Fernbedienung*
to remove	*entfernen*
rent	*Miete*
to rent	*mieten*
to repair	*reparieren*
to repeat	*wiederholen*
to reply	*antworten*
reputation	*Ruf*
request	*Anfrage, Bitte*
reservation	*Reservierung*
residence	*Aufenthalt; (am Telefon) Familie*
resort	*Badeort*
to rest	*sich ausruhen*
resume	*Lebenslauf*
to retire	*in Rente gehen*
to return	*zurückkehren*
return ticket	*Rückfahrkarte*
to reveal	*enthüllen*
rice	*Reis*
to ride	*mit etw. fahren, reiten*
right	*direkt; (nach) rechts; richtig*
right behind sb.	*direkt hinter jdm.*
to ring	*klingeln*
river	*Fluss*
road	*Straße*
road sign	*Straßenschild*
roll	*Brötchen*
romantic	*romantisch*
roof	*Dach*
room	*Raum, Zimmer*
roundabout	*Kreisverkehr*
rucksack	*Rucksack*
rug	*Teppich*
rule	*Regel*
to run	*rennen*
to run away	*wegrennen*
rush job	*hektische Angelegenheit*
Russia	*Russland*
Russian	*russisch; Russe/n, Russin*

S

sad	*traurig*
sadness	*Traurigkeit*
to sail	*segeln*
sale	*Ausverkauf*
sales	*Verkauf*
salesperson	*Verkäufer/in*
salon	*Salon, Studio (Friseur)*
salt	*Salz*
same	*gleich/e/r/s*
sandwich	*Sandwich, belegtes Brot*
Saturday	*Samstag*
Saudi Arabia	*Saudi Arabien*
sausage	*Wurst*
savage	*wild*
to save	*speichern*
savoury	*herzhaft*
saw	*Säge*
to say	*sagen*
Say what now?	*Wie bitte? (informell)*
scared	*verängstigt, erschrocken*
to scare s.o.	*jdn. erschrecken*
scarf	*Schal*
scholarship	*Stipendium*
school	*Schule*
science	*(Natur-)Wissenschaft*
scientist	*Naturwissenschaftler/in*
scoop	*Kugel (Eis)*
Scotland	*Schottland*
Scottish	*schottisch; Schotte/n, Schottin*
scout	*Pfadfinder*
scream	*Schrei, Aufschrei*
to scream	*schreien*
screen	*Bildschirm*
screw	*Schraube*
sea	*Meer*
sea level	*Meeresspiegel*
to search	*(nach etw.) suchen*
seaside	*am Meer/See (gelegen)*
seaside town	*Küstenstädtchen*
seat	*Sitz, Platz*
seatbelt	*Gurt*
second	*Sekunde; zweiter*
secret	*Geheimnis*
to see	*sehen*
to seem to do sth.	*scheinbar etw. tun*
to seem very strange	*äußerst seltsam erscheinen*
selection	*Auswahl*
to sell	*verkaufen*
semester	*Semester*
to send	*schicken, senden*
sentence	*Satz*
September	*September*
serious	*ernst*
to serve	*servieren, bedienen*
to serve lunch	*das Mittagessen servieren*
to set up	*etw. aufbauen*
seven	*sieben*
seventh	*der / die / das siebte*
seventy	*siebzig*
several	*mehrere, einige*
to shake (one's head)	*(den Kopf) schütteln*
shall we	*sollen wir*
she	*sie*

sheet	*Blatt; hier: Lasagneplatte (aus Nudelteig)*
shelf	*Regal*
shirt	*Hemd*
shoe	*Schuh*
shop	*Laden*
to shop	*einkaufen*
short	*kurz*
shortly	*kurz*
shorts	*Shorts*
should	*sollte*
shoulder	*Schulter*
to show	*zeigen*
to show up	*auftauchen, erscheinen*
shower	*Dusche*
to shut down	*ausschalten (Rechner)*
shy	*scheu*
sick	*krank; übel*
side	*Seite*
sight	*Sehenswürdigkeit*
to sightsee	*Sehenswürdigkeiten besuchen*
sign	*Schild*
to sign	*unterschreiben*
to sign in	*einloggen*
signal	*Signal*
silent	*ruhig, still*
silhouette	*Silhouette*
to simmer	*köcheln*
simple	*einfach*
simply	*einfach*
since	*seit (Zeitpunkt)*
Singapore	*Singapur*
to sing	*singen*
single	*ledig; einzeln*
single room	*Einzelzimmer*
to sink	*sinken*
sink	*Waschbecken; Spüle*
sister	*Schwester*
to sit down	*sich hinsetzen*
to sit on	*sitzen auf*
situation	*Situation*
six	*sechs*
sixth	*der / die / das Sechste*
sixty	*sechzig*
size	*Größe*
to ski	*Ski fahren*
skin	*Haut*
skinny	*dünn, mager*
skirt	*Rock*
sky	*Himmel*
skyline	*Skyline, Silhouette*
skyscraper	*Wolkenkratzer*
to sleep	*schlafen*
sleeping bag	*Schlafsack*
slice	*Stück, Scheibe*
to slice	*in Scheiben schneiden*
slight	*schwach, leicht*
slim	*schlank*
to slip	*ausrutschen*

Slovakia	*die Slowakei*
slow	*langsam*
to slow	*langsamer werden*
small	*klein*
smart	*hier: schick*
smell	*Geruch*
smile	*Lächeln*
to smile	*lächeln*
to smoke	*rauchen*
sneakers (AE)	*Turnschuhe*
to sneeze	*niesen*
to snow	*schneien*
snow	*Schnee*
snowflake	*Schneeflocke*
snowplough	*Schneepflug*
so	*also*
sock	*Socke*
sofa	*Sofa*
so far, so good	*so weit, so gut*
soft	*weich*
to solve	*lösen*
some	*einige, etwas*
someone	*jemand*
something	*etwas*
sometimes	*manchmal*
son	*Sohn*
song	*Lied*
soon	*bald*
sorry	*Entschuldigung*
sort of	*Art von*
sound	*Geräusch, Klang*
to sound	*klingen*
Sounds like a plan!	*Klingt gut!*
soup	*Suppe*
soup plate	*Suppenteller*
south	*südlich, nach Süden*
South	*Süden*
South Africa	*Südafrika*
Spain	*Spanien*
Spanish	*spanisch*
to speak	*sprechen*
special	*besondere/r/s*
specifically	*spezifisch*
speech	*Rede*
to spend	*verbringen*
spicy	*scharf*
splendid	*großartig, brillant, herrlich*
spoon	*Löffel*
sport	*Sport*
sports car	*Sportwagen*
spot	*Platz*
sprained	*verstaucht*
spring	*Frühling*
stairs	*Treppen*
to stand	*stehen*
to stand up	*aufstehen*
star	*Stern*
to start	*anfangen*
station	*Station, Haltestelle*

to stay	*bleiben*
to stay away from sth./sb.	*sich von etw./jdm. fernhalten*
to step	*treten*
step	*Schritt, Stufe*
still	*immer noch*
to stir	*rühren*
stomach	*Bauch; Magen*
stomachache	*Bauchschmerzen*
stone	*Stein*
stone path	*Steinpfad*
stone wall	*Steinmauer*
to stop	*anhalten, aufhören*
storage room	*Speisekammer, Lagerraum*
store	*Laden*
storm	*Sturm*
story	*Geschichte*
stove	*Herd*
straight	*gerade*
strange	*seltsam*
stranger	*Fremde/r*
strawberry	*Erdbeere*
street	*Straße*
stripe	*Streife*
stronger	*stärker/e/r/s*
stuff	*Sachen, Zeug*
stunning	*umwerfend*
to struggle	*sich abmühen; mit etw. kämpfen*
student	*Student/-in*
stuffed	*voll sein*
stupid	*dumm*
style	*Stil*
success	*Erfolg*
successful	*erfolgreich*
suddenly	*plötzlich*
sugar	*Zucker*
suit	*Anzug*
suitcase	*Koffer*
summary	*Zusammenfassung*
summer	*Sommer*
to summon	*herbeirufen*
sun	*Sonne*
to sunbathe	*sich bräunen*
Sunday	*Sonntag*
sunglasses (Pl.)	*Sonnenbrille*
sunny	*sonnig*
sunny-side up	*Spiegelei*
to suppose	*annehmen*
surcharge	*Aufpreis*
sure	*sicher*
surname	*Nachname*
surprise	*Überraschung*
Sweden	*Schweden*
sweet	*süß*
sweetie	*Süße (Kosename)*
sweets	*Süßigkeiten*
to swim	*schwimmen*
Swiss	*schweizerisch; Schweizer/in*
Switzerland	*die Schweiz*
syrup	*Sirup*
T	
T-shirt	*T-Shirt*
table	*Tisch*
tablet	*Tablet(computer)*
to take	*nehmen; dauern*
Take care!	*Mach(t)'s gut!*
to take care of sth.	*sich um etw. kümmern*
to take a picture	*ein Bild machen*
to take over	*übernehmen*
to take sb out	*jmdn einladen, jmdn ausführen*
to talk	*sprechen, sich unterhalten*
tall	*groß*
to taste	*schmecken, kosten*
tasty	*lecker, schmackhaft*
tax	*Steuer*
taxi driver	*Taxifahrer/-in*
tea	*Tee*
teacher	*Lehrer/in*
to teach	*lehren*
tear	*Träne*
teenager	*Teenager*
teeth (Pl.)	*Zähne*
television screen	*Fernsehbildschirm*
to tell	*erzählen*
telly (BE)	*Fernseher (informell)*
ten	*zehn*
tent	*Zelt*
tenth	*der/die/das zehnte*
terrible	*schrecklich*
terrified	*verängstigt*
terrifying	*furchteinflößend*
to text	*simsen*
textile	*Textil*
than	*als*
thank you	*danke*
that	*das*
that is all	*das war's schon*
the other day	*letztens*
them	*sie, ihnen*
then	*dann*
there	*dort*
they	*sie*
thin	*dünn*
thing	*Ding, Sache*
to think	*denken*
third	*dritte/r/s*
thirsty	*durstig*
thirty	*dreißig*
this time	*dieses Mal*
those	*jene*
thousand	*Tausend*
three	*drei*
through	*durch (hindurch)*
to throw	*werfen*

to throw away sth.	*etwas wegwerfen*
thunder	*Donner*
thunderstorm	*Gewitter*
Thursday	*Donnerstag*
ticket	*(Fahr-)Karte*
tidy	*ordentlich, aufgeräumt*
to tidy (up)	*aufräumen*
tie	*Krawatte, Schlips*
tight	*eng*
time	*Zeit; Mal*
tiny	*winzig*
tip	*Tipp; Trinkgeld*
title	*Titel*
to	*zu, nach*
today	*heute*
toe	*Zeh*
together	*zusammen*
toilet	*Toilette*
tomato (pl. tomatoes)	*Tomate*
tomato paste	*Tomatenmark*
tomorrow	*morgen*
tonight	*heute Abend*
too	*zu (+ Adjektiv)*
tool	*Werkzeug*
top	*Spitze*
top honours	*Spitzennoten*
to torch	*Fackel*
torso	*Oberkörper*
touch	*anfassen, berühren*
touched	*bewegt*
tour	*Rundgang, Tour*
touristy	*touristenmäßig*
towards	*in Richtung von*
tower	*Turm*
town	*Stadt*
town hall	*Rathaus*
traditional	*traditionell*
traffic light	*Ampel*
trail	*Pfad*
train	*Zug*
trainers	*Turnschuhe*
train station	*Bahnhof*
tram	*Straßenbahn*
to transfer	*etw. von einem Ort zum anderen bewegen*
trash	*Abfall, Müll*
to travel	*reisen*
travel agency	*Reisebüro*
travel guide	*Reiseführer (Buch)*
to treat sb (to sth)	*jmdn einladen (auswärts essen)*
tree	*Baum*
trillion	*Trillion*
trip	*Reise*
to trip	*stolpern*
trouble	*Schwierigkeiten; Umstände*
trousers	*Hose*
true	*wahr*
trumpet	*Trompete*
to trust sb	*jmdm. vertrauen*
to try	*versuchen*
to try sth. on	*etw. anprobieren*
to try sth. out	*etw. ausprobieren*
Tube	*U-Bahn (London)*
Tuesday	*Dienstag*
tunnel	*Tunnel*
turkey	*Pute; Truthahn*
Turkey	*die Türkei*
to turn (an age)	*(ein Alter) werden*
to turn (around)	*sich (um)drehen*
to turn off	*abschalten*
to turn on sth	*etwas einschalten*
turn out	*sich herausstellen*
turtleneck	*Rollkragenpullover*
twelve	*zwölf*
twenty	*zwanzig*
twice	*zweimal*
to twist	*verdrehen, verrenken*
two	*zwei*
typical	*typisch*
U	
ugly	*hässlich*
unbeatable	*unschlagbar*
under	*unter*
underground	*U-Bahn*
underneath	*unter*
to understand	*verstehen*
unfashionable	*unmodisch*
unfortunately	*unglücklicherweise, leider*
unhappy	*traurig, unglücklich*
United Kingdom	*Vereinigtes Königreich*
United States of America	*Vereinigte Staaten von Amerika*
university	*Universität*
unless	*wenn nicht*
to untie	*lösen, losmachen*
until	*bis*
up	*auf, hinauf*
up-to-date	*aktuell, auf dem neuesten Stand*
us	*uns*
to use	*benutzen*
username	*Benutzername*
usually	*gewöhnlich*
V	
to vacuum	*staubsaugen*
vacuum cleaner	*Staubsauger*
validation	*Bestätigung*
valley	*Tal*
vegetables	*Gemüse*
very	*sehr*
veterinarian	*Tierarzt, Tierärztin*
veterinary medicine	*Tiermedizin*
view	*Sicht, Ausblick*
village	*Dorf*
vintage car	*Klassiker (Auto), Oldtimer*
violin	*Geige*

	visit	*besuchen*
	voice	*Stimme*

W

to	wait	*warten*
	waiting room	*Wartezimmer*
to	wake sb. (up)	*jdn. wecken*
to	wake up	*aufwachen*
	Wales	*Wales*
	walk	*Spaziergang*
to	walk	*gehen*
	wall	*Wand; Mauer*
to	wallet (AE)	*Geldbeutel*
to	want	*wollen*
	warm	*warm*
to	warm	*aufwärmen*
to	warn	*warnen*
to	wash	*waschen*
	washing machine	*Waschmaschine*
to	waste	*verschwenden*
	watch	*Armbanduhr*
to	watch	*beobachten, schauen*
to	watch television	*fernsehen*
	water	*Wasser*
to	water sth	*gießen*
	way	*Weg; Art, Weise*
	we	*wir*
	weak	*schwach*
to	wear	*tragen (Kleidung)*
	weather	*Wetter*
	wedding	*Hochzeit*
	wedding anniversary	*Hochzeitstag*
	Wednesday	*Mittwoch*
	week	*Woche*
	weekend	*Wochenende*
to	welcome	*Willkommen*
	welcome sb.	*jdn. willkommen heißen*
	welcoming	*freundlich*
	welder	*Schweißer/in*
	Well, ...	*Also, ...; Äh, ...*
	Welsh	*walisisch*
	west	*westlich, nach Westen*
	West	*Westen*
	wet	*nass*
	what	*was*
	whatever	*was auch immer*
	what on earth	*was um Himmels willen, was zum Teufel*
	What's wrong?	*Was ist los?*
	wheelchair	*Rollstuhl*
	when	*wenn, sobald; als*
	where	*wo*
	wherever	*wo auch immer*
	whether	*ob*
to	which	*der/die/das, welche/r/s*
	while	*während*
	whipped cream	*Schlagsahne*
	whisper	*flüstern*
	white	*weiß*
	who	*wer, wen, wem*
	whom	*wen, wem*
	why	*warum*
	wife	*Ehefrau*
	wig	*Perücke*
	will	*werden*
	wind	*Wind*
	window	*Fenster*
to	windscreen	*Windschutzscheibe*
to	win	*gewinnen*
	wine	*Wein*
	winner	*Sieger/-in, Gewinner/-in*
	winter	*Winter*
	winter coat	*Mantel*
	wire	*Draht*
	wish	*Wunsch*
to	wish	*wünschen*
	Wish me luck!	*Drück mir die Daumen!*
	with	*mit*
	within	*innerhalb*
	without	*ohne*
	woman (pl. women)	*Frau*
to	wonder	*sich fragen*
	wonderful	*wunderbar*
	work	*Arbeit*
to	work	*arbeiten*
to	work out	*trainieren, Sport machen*
	world	*Welt*
	worried	*besorgt*
to	worry	*sich sorgen*
	worse	*schlimmer/e/r/s*
	worst	*schlimmste/r/s*
	would like	*möchten*
to	wrap sth. up	*etwas zum Schluss bringen*
	write	*schreiben*
	writer	*Autor/in*
	wrong	*falsch*

Y

yard	*Yard (Längenmaß ca. 1 m)*
yeah	*ja (informell)*
year	*Jahr*
yellow	*gelb*
yes	*ja*
yesterday	*gestern*
yoghurt	*Joghurt*
you	*du, dich, dir, Sie, Ihnen, ihr, euch*
You can say that again!	*Das kannst du laut sagen!*
young	*jung*
your	*dein/e, eur/e, ihr/e, Ihr/e,*

Z

zebra crossing	*Zebrastreifen*